INSCRIBE CHRISTIAN WRITERS' FELLOWSHIP

Christmas

Stories & More

Press

Christmas: Stories & More

Copyright © 2017 by InScribe Press

Cover design: Ellen Hooge www.siretona.com
Interior illustrations, design, and formatting: Ellen Hooge
E-book Design: Wild Seas Formatting www.WildSeasFormatting.com

Cover Photo: Da Puglet / Boo the Pug / Creative Commons / Flickr
Photo: pg 26 / Ruth L. Snyder
Photo: pg 54 / Sally Meadows
Photo: pg 97 / provided by M. Eleanor Maisey
Image: pg 99 / provided by Jack D. Popjes
Photo: pg 115 / John Morgan / Aidan decorates the tree / CC / Flickr
Photo: pg 141 / US Army / contest 110311 / CC / Flickr
Photo: pg 165 / Ruth L. Snyder
Photo: pg 171 / Pat Gerbrandt
Photo: pg 185 / Wendy L. Macdonald

Published by InScribe Press https://inscribe.org.
Printed by PageMaster Publishing:https://pagemasterpublishing.ca
ISBN: 978-0-9940405-2-7

Endorsements

Christmas: Stories & More is a collection of inspirational writing by authors from all across Canada. Stories are of the very young and the very old, of rich families and poor, and of Christmas past and present. Tales are woven of hearts frozen by guilt, sorrow, and loneliness, and warmed by the love of family, friends, and the message of God's love for a broken world through the gift of His Son, Jesus.

These are stories that you will want to share with others, reading them aloud to your family, or giving the entire collection as a gift to someone you love.

- Dorene Meyer, author of *The Little Ones*

The writers of InScribe have given us a very special book. The writing is exceptional and the stories that their writing brings to life are just as exceptional. This book is not just enjoyable but inspirational in a very real way. There is something about Christmas that can bring out either the best in writers or some of the overly sentimental worst. In this case, we have the best—a book that makes a difference not just at Christmas but all year round.

- Murray Pura, author of *The Wings of Morning, A Road Called Love,* and *An Amish Family Christmas.*

Table Of Contents

Foreword

Christmas.
This single word has the power to recreate an atmosphere
and conjure up a host of memories. Snatches of Christmas
carols, the spicy scent of a spruce tree, the snap of Christmas
cookies. The flicker of candles and the glow from a fire.
Chubby fingers tearing at shiny red paper, bright eyes and
squeals of delight at gifts that had been yearned for and
now received. Christmas is like an entity unto itself with
cards, trees, music, sweaters, decorations, recipes,
books, and movies all devoted to this single word. This
single season.

Christmas.
The word Christmas as well, carries a weight—the weight
of expectations and traditions. It can, conversely, carry the
weight of sorrow. It is a time when the empty spaces at the
table can stretch larger. When losses can darken even the
brightest lights.

Christmas.
This single word takes so much along with it. Home for
Christmas. A deadline, a waiting, an expectation. It can be a
blessing for some, an obligation for others, and a dread for
yet others.

In this collection of fictional and real-life stories, poems,
plays, and recipes, you will see Christmas through other
eyes. You will read stories of grace: an invasion of

Christmas carollers, angels in disguise, Christmas in a jungle, and Christ found in the unlikeliest of places. You will read poems that make us all yearn for more than the small taste of eternity that comes to us at Christmas, and experience the thoughts of wise men who sought the same thing we do in this season of expectations. Light. Peace. Grace. Love. As you read these stories, you will feel the anticipation, experience the traditions, and recognize that no matter how hard we've worked and prepared and shopped, something better, brighter, and more beautiful lies just beyond our reach.

I hope you enjoy this collection of plays, poems, reflections, and stories. I pray you may, through these authors' words, see the hope that Christmas brings. A hope that will still the restlessness that resonates through our lives. A hope that brings us peace on earth and promises a better peace for the future.

- Carolyn Aarsen

Introduction

  This book is literally a voluntary labour of love. It started with the seed of an idea, planted by InScribe Executive members. Sally Meadows volunteered to be our InScribe Press "master gardener," gathering information, putting together a call for submissions, and searching for able and willing helpers. The selection team spent hours poring over almost one hundred submissions and paring them down to fifty-six exemplary pieces. Then professional editors, who are members of InScribe, nurtured and pruned the chosen submissions. After that, Sally carefully placed each piece in a suitable location and combination, and nurtured and pruned it some more until it was as polished as possible.

  Ellen Hooge then designed the beautiful layout, preparing it for printing. Sally and others worked on getting the book distributed in Canada and beyond. I extend my sincere thanks to each person who donated time and expertise to make this book a reality.

  InScribe Christian Writers' Fellowship welcomes your feedback. You can connect with individual authors using the information provided in the Biographies section at the back of the book. Book reviews may be shared on Amazon and Goodreads. Suggestions for upcoming anthologies can be sent to Press@inscribe.org. If you are a writer, we encourage you to join us at https://inscribe.org/membership.

Sincerely,

Ruth L. Snyder
President
InScribe Christian Writers' Fellowship

Christmas in Kharkiv
1932

by Pamela Mytroen

Dmitri huddled in the trees, holding his breath in the misty Christmas morning. He waited for the vegetable wagon to hit the small hole he had dug in the road. Would it be enough to free a large cabbage? Even a small beet? The wagon tipped. It shuddered under the weight of its precious cargo but refused to release anything. He scanned the road. Still no uniforms.

Dmitri swallowed and spit out blood. Eating nettles had blistered his lips and throat. He tried to pray again but why bother? God never listened. He had abandoned him, and left him to his fists to fight for food. He clenched his fingers, still swollen from his last scuffle. Was the moldy onion he won from that young man worth the blows he gave him? He shook his guilt away. If there were another battle today, he would win. He must.

Thud! A knobby potato landed on the snow-packed road and rolled along a rut. Dmitri's mouth watered. He dug his boots into the snow, preparing to sprint.

"Hurry," he whispered, willing the driver to keep moving. He stood and squinted at the patch of snow that held life.

Movement caught his eye. He ducked and peered through the branches. Instead of a man in uniform, it was the neighbour girl. She was running with her long black curls flying straight out behind her. He yanked on the leash of his hunger, holding back for a second. *A girl? If I hurry there will be no fight. And no extra guilt to carry.* Dmitri

10

sprang from safety and raced, but she was just as quick. Their hands met in a tangle on the Christmas potato.

"Mine!" she said, sinking her nails into it.

Dmitri wrestled the potato towards his chest and fell back. The girl held her grip and landed on his bony ribs. A new hunger pinched Dmitri's stomach. "You've grown, Natalia."

She fixed her sky-blue eyes on the potato and tugged it to her chest. "I'm starving."

"We could share." He pulled the potato back his way. "This would last both of us three days."

Her shoulders relaxed a little, but she stiffened again and yanked the potato her way.

If he were willing to share, would God forgive his calloused heart? "I have enough wood for a fire," said Dmitri. "Roasted or boiled? Which do you like better, Natalia?"

He would give her all the time she needed to answer. Her dark curls danced like a glissando of music notes against the snow, and the press of her warmth against his empty belly hushed his hunger, encouraging other thoughts besides the constant longing for food.

"If you eat, you will just get hungry again," said Natalia. Smiling at him, she ripped away from Dmitri with the potato intact in her red hands and shimmied backwards until she managed to get to her feet.

Dmitri reached her in two of his long-legged strides and caged her in his arms. She elbowed him in the side and ducked under his arm. "Not fast enough are you Dmitri!" She ran backwards and taunted him with the potato above her head.

Dmitri would not eat nettles again. Not when he was this close to real food. He charged and caught her for the second time. "I can play this game all day," he said. But the sharp tone in his voice betrayed his hunger as he held her small elbows in a fierce grip.

She challenged him with her steady gaze. "The

Klymchuks are cold in their graves," she said. Dmitri glanced at the farmyard down the road. A gray shroud hovered over the trees. "And the Yovenkos and the Liskis. Even the children are gone." Her voice rose in pitch. "And look what this has done to us." She dropped her gaze to the potato between them. "We used to be friends. And now we fight." Shame, hardened by hunger, pulsed in the gentle curve of her jaw.

Death had visited Dmitri's home too. It had lullabied its way into their family, first in the weakness of his once-strong father, and then in the swollen bellies of his mother and brothers, and finally it had wailed a shrieking vigil as one by one they lost their minds. He had fought off the neurosis, digging in waste piles for vegetable peels, weeds, . . . anything.

And now death hovered as the referee between Natalia and Dmitri. They both looked at the potato. One would live today. And one would go insane.

Dmitri sucked in a mouth full of shocking cold and resolved to hang on. He would not allow this girl to break him. But she was a fighter, too. A memory lit his mind like a falling star. It was the time she had squealed on him when he had cheated on his high school assessments. He had been disqualified for university. She had been accepted, and enjoyed the softer life of the city. Dmitri's thumbs pushed into her forearms.

As if she read his mind, she hung her head and breathed out slowly. "I do not deserve to live." He felt the rise and fall of her tiny shoulders. "Your brother . . . it was my fault."

"What?" Disbelief dizzied him.

"They offered me food, Dmitri. All I had to do was name one person. One enemy."

"My brother an enemy? He only hid a little grain. How could you?"

"They gave us enough to eat for a week."

12

He looked into her pleading eyes and all he could see were his brother's. Anger fired up his guilt, sparking new resolve. If an educated girl could betray his family, then surely he could get away with stealing. Dmitri could be greedy without conscience. If God didn't answer his prayers, what did He expect?

"You will give me the potato, then," said Dmitri evenly. "It is the least you can do." He slid his hands forward on her arms until his thumbs pinned the potato.

Natalia reddened, but hung on. "Dmitri. Please. I am sorry. We were so hungry." She squeezed her eyes shut. Long black lashes laid down in rows. "My sisters . . . I left university to come home and save them. I promised them, Dmitri. But they have all died. I betrayed them too." She bit her lip. "And I have been to all the neighbour's homes." She looked aside. Fear lined her forehead. "I have—"

"Quiet! He released her arms and pressed his fingers against her lips. He tried to quiet his own thoughts, too, but they circled like vultures, around and around. He remembered the child clutching a stolen handful of barley. Dmitri had peeled each kernel from his bony fingers, one by one. And the mother holding her baby, watching Dmitri with vacant eyes as he shook her tree and claimed her last three apples. "Please do not say any more. What you confess, it condemns me as well." He too had done the despicable just to survive. Dmitri caved under his own darkness, a broken raven in the snow.

Lord? Do You hear me? Will You forgive me? Silence from the skies sifted into his soul. Again. But this time he felt cleansed. And Dmitri knew what he must do.

He shook his head. He pushed his fists into his aching stomach. Closed his eyes. *Give me strength.*

Dmitri slipped off one glove and rubbed Natalia's red fingers on the potato until they warmed under his thumb. He raised her chin to look at him.

"I thought God had forgotten me." He caressed the

guilt from her cheeks until they softened with her tears.

"But you have brought Christmas to me, Natalia. I hear it in your confession. Your heart is still soft." The wind howled a circle of snow around them. "I am starving too, but my heart is far more empty than my belly." Natalia's chin quivered and Dmitri searched for her eyes, but she refused to meet his. He pressed on before he changed his mind. "I need to be filled again. God gave us Jesus. He will fill me. I need Him to live. To really live."

Natalia said nothing. He tore his hopeful gaze away from the meal in her hand. "Christ was born so that I could be forgiven." He folded his hands over hers on the potato, and pushed it back to her. "So that I could show grace."

She looked up at him, sighed, and bowed her head. Dmitri bowed too, and accepted the sweet taste of mercy. It poured over him and filled him, and the glacier of guilt cracked and crumbled and began to fall away.

"Are you going to stand here all day, or cook that for dinner?" Dmitri smiled, hoping for a smile of hers in return, a last supper. Natalia's jaw twitched and she clutched the prize closer.

Dmitri looked away from the food. "Let me know how it tastes, will you?"

"It will taste stolen," she said in frosty breath. "Stolen from Stalin."

"Not stolen," he whispered, weak from the run. "It is sent. Sent from Heaven." He squeezed her shoulder, backed up a step, and turned around to face the cold catacomb of home.

A crunch-crunch sounded behind him. He forced his hands into his pockets, knowing.

"Wanna bite?"

Dmitri did not turn. Natalia came around to face him. Her fine-boned chin challenged him with the potato between her teeth. She grinned and wiped a salt-and-pepper-trail of potato and dirt from her chin. "It's good."

Dmitri folded his arms. He had no more energy for another game. She held the potato with its fresh white scar under his nose. He cemented his gaze, but how could he harden himself against the girl who had been the first to confess? He leaned down. She pulled away and giggled.

"Where's that potato?" A woman called. "Natalia?" She called again, snapping out each syllable of her name. Natalia tossed Dmitri the giant spud. It smacked him in the chest and he fumbled it, tossing it from hand to hand until he finally secured it between his gloves.

"Come for dinner," said Natalia. "We're roasting our last hen."

"A hen?" Dmitri lowered his voice. "How?"

"I raised it in the house." Her laugh sang like the stream by the mill.

Dmitri whooped. A sharp crack turned his joy to terror. Natalia paled. Dmitri dropped the potato and toed snow over it. But it was only a line of clothes snapping in the wind. Dmitri fell to his knees in relief and retrieved the contraband, slipping it in his pocket.

"What will your mother say?" he asked as he stood and reached for Natalia's hand. "Sounds like she's expecting you. And the potato."

She only offered a sideways grin.

"I suppose she can't be any meaner than you," he said, worrying the potato around in his pocket.

She kicked him hard in the shin and bolted, but this time he wasn't letting go of her, or the dinner.

Natalia rushed Dmitri up the stone stairway and into a dark but warm kitchen. She whispered to her mother. His knees buckled at the aroma of fresh bread.

Natalia's mother prodded her bony hands into Dmitri's side, demanding the potato. When she saw the bite-mark, she slapped the potato on the counter and fastened her hands on her ample hips, sentencing him with her grey eyes. He stopped breathing and dared a sideways glance

15

at Natalia. He should have known the feisty girl would wink. The woman inspected Dmitri's gaunt frame and baggy clothes, frowning at the big toe that had pushed its way out from his boot.

He shifted. Removed his gloves. Put them back on. Finally, he remembered his manners. "Christ is born, Mrs. Danachevsky."

Mrs. Danachevsky reached for the potato, and weighed it back and forth, back and forth. Hope teetered between her hands.

Lord? Do You ration grace?

Mrs. Danachevsky divvied out one careful scowl to Dmitri, one fork, and one whispered command to her daughter. "Natalia? An extra plate. Christ is born today!"

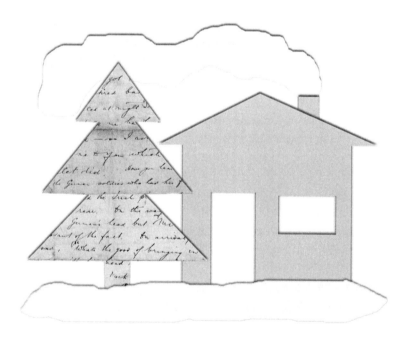

Street Kid

by

Kathleen Friesen

A bitter December wind chilled Mitch's bones, matching his mood as he trudged towards the mission. *They'll have good food there, especially this close to Christmas*, he thought. He pulled his hoodie string tighter and rubbed his face with both hands. If only he could grow a beard like Jackson's.

"Just wait a few years, it'll come," his mom had said.

He didn't want to think about Mom.

Mitch pulled the door open. "Joy To The World" struck him like a slap in the face, but he softened when he realized it was just little kids singing. Harmless. About a dozen middle school kids stood in a semi-circle, their faces shiny, their clothes clean. One boy stood out. He was taller than the others, and his dark, wavy hair, wide cheeks, and brown eyes reminded Mitch of himself at that age. Before…

Time reversed to six months ago, to his mom and their last argument. He'd yelled words he now wished he could take back. He'd filled his backpack and met his best friend, Jackson, at the highway. Hitching rides, they'd escaped from their small Saskatchewan town to Vancouver, where they were sure all their dreams would come true. Fast-forward past soul-numbing humiliations, Jackson's drug use and their fights about it, to the sight Mitch couldn't forget. His friend, dead of an overdose.

They'd sought utopia and freedom from rules, and instead found death.

The kids switched to "O Holy Night." Mom's

favourite. Mitch's chest ached as he remembered decorating their spindly tree together one Christmas, laughing as he stretched to place the angel on top. Good times, back then. He could almost hear her say, "I love you," and—the last couple years—watch her smile fade as she waited for him to say it back.

He leaned against the wall as a man walked to the front, his back straight and white hair gleaming under the lights. He began to speak, and Mitch tuned out, fighting memories. The familiar Christmas story seemed no more than background noise until Mitch looked up and saw the man looking right at him. "Jesus left the glory of Heaven for this dirty, cruel world, to save you. No matter what you've done, He loves you." As the man wrapped up, Mitch replayed the words over and over in his head. "He loves you."

The guy bowed his head and said some words. Mitch shuffled his feet as he waited for the "amen" so he could line up for the hot meal. It smelled like turkey. His stomach rumbled loudly.

A few minutes later, Mitch set his full plate on the table and pulled out a chair. But before he could sit, a hand landed on his shoulder. He spun around and faced the white-haired preacher.

"Mind if I join you?"

What could he say? "Yeah, okay."

The man sat beside Mitch without violating his space and waited while Mitch quickly consumed the turkey, potatoes, gravy, and even the mixed vegetables. Staring at his empty plate, Mitch relished the rare sensation of hunger satisfied.

The man cleared his throat, and Mitch reluctantly faced him. He didn't want to talk, but with his stomach full and his body warm, he couldn't force himself to leave.

The man's eyes glowed as he spoke softly. "Where you from, son?"

Mitch started to tell him to mind his own business,

but instead, his whole sorry tale poured out. How he'd rebelled, thought he was so smart. How he'd mouthed off to his mom until their home had become unbearable. Now, their tiny apartment seemed like a palace, warm and welcoming. How could he have been so dumb?

The preacher pulled out his phone. "Jesus loves you, son, and your mom does, too. Call her."

Mitch stared at him for several heartbeats. Finally, he took a deep breath, and with shaking fingers, made the call.

It only rang once before his mom's wary "Hello?" filled his ear.

Another deep, shaky breath. "Hey, Mom, it's me. Merry Christmas."

"Mitch!" Then sobs muffled her words. "Where…? Are you okay? Please, son—please come home. I love you so much."

"I'd like that, Mom." He swallowed hard and closed his eyes. "I—I love you, too."

"For the Son of Man came to seek and to save the lost" *(Luke 19:10).*

The Carol

by

Gloria Guest

Mary stared at the carollers on her front porch. She had begrudgingly opened the door for them this frigid winter's night, but now she wished them away.

Did they not have anything better to do than to sing in the cold? Could they not go and interrupt someone else's night? Not that she had been doing much, but at least she hadn't been feeling as irritated as she was now.

There was annoying Ann from next door, bundled up, looking like a ridiculous singing snowman. Mary knew Ann wouldn't care how silly she looked and that fact irritated her even more. Too bad it wasn't warmer and Ann would just melt away.

And there was Al, a widower she had met recently. He seemed nice enough but Mary couldn't help but be suspicious of him. Well, in reality, she acknowledged she was suspicious of everyone. It always took her a while to accept new people, or to feel comfortable enough to say hello at the post office. Which to Mary was far more than enough to be friendly. People always thought they needed to stop and chat. Mary didn't care to chat. She'd much rather be on her way, back to her cozy home at the end of the street and to her two cats, Milly and Tom. They were all the company she needed. But right now, upon hearing strange voices, the cats had abandoned her for a secluded spot in the house. Lucky them.

Mary shivered in her flimsy housecoat, embarrassed that she hadn't been wearing something a little more appropriate when she opened the door. But it had been too late to pretend she wasn't home. She was sure they had all seen her peering out the window, her face showing strong displeasure when she saw the dozen or so people stomping onto her front porch. It was a veritable crowd. And then, without further warning, they had begun belting out the words to "Joy to the World."

Mary felt glad for the cold reddening her face. It would hide the rush of embarrassment creeping up her neck. So many eyes on her. And singing! How was she supposed to react? Should she at least try to look happy? It was all too much. She took a step back in retreat and immediately regretted it. The leader of the group, Mildred, the church organist from the local Baptist church, seemed to take Mary's step back as an invitation to move forward. And then, before she knew it, the whole lot of them, as if in practiced unison, had moved forward with her. And then, well, what could she do when Al with his frosted-over moustache said, "I'm freezing. Let's just step inside for one moment. Mary won't mind will ya?"

Mary did mind. But it was like fighting a tidal wave. "I agree," a shivering lady said as she pushed past Al into the front entrance. And then it was nothing but commotion with the stomping of snow from boots, the whoosh of unzipping of jackets, requests for Kleenexes, and the loud blowing of noses. Mary was sure someone had rushed off to use the bathroom. How rude. Mary stood back and surveyed the disruptive group. She did seem to at least know them all. But still. Was this supposed to feel nice?

And then, while Mary stood watching with a look of strained patience on her face, they organized themselves again.

"Thank you so much, Mary, for your kindness towards our carollers," Mildred said. "Could we sing you just one more song before we go, to thank you?"

"Oh no, no. It's really not necessary," Mary

stammered, but Frank in the back belted out in his nasal voice, "I know just the one," and started them off.

It was a song she hadn't heard before, but her ears perked up as the song started off with her own name.

"Mary, Did You Know?"* The most melancholy, yet oddly hopeful words wound their way through the music, straight into her heart. A song that talked about a baby boy walking on water; the blind seeing and the lame leaping; and the dead living again.

Mary's hand flew to her wildly beating heart. Mary's boy. Her boy. Her own beautiful son. Tears pricked at her eyes as she remembered the first time she'd heard the awful news. The uniformed men had stood on her porch on a cold night very much like this one, and had asked to be invited in. They were dressed just like her Luke used to be. And she had invited them in and then would forever wish she hadn't. Their horrid words had turned her world upside down, and left her with nothing.

"We're very sorry to inform you ma'am...."

Luke was eight years old when he first painted his face that horrid, putrid green and told her that he wanted to join the army. Mary had sent him to Sunday school with a friend, thinking that God would change his mind. She fought against the idea for many years, but her husband Jack had not. Rather, he seemed to encourage the boy, arguing that she had to let her growing boy live his life. Her husband allowed Luke to join Cadets and play war games on the computer. And then, in the end, it didn't seem to matter what either of them thought because their strong, independent, now eighteen-year-old had gone and signed up the day after his high school graduation, right as the war in Afghanistan was beginning. Luke said he'd felt peace, like it was God's plan for him, but a bitter seed had begun to grow within Mary's heart. God had failed her. And so had Jack.

Eventually, after those men had come with the

news that Luke would not be coming home, Jack had left too. Mary knew that he blamed himself and she had done nothing to assuage his guilt. Her heart had turned as frozen as the winter night when the news had come and she had offered her husband no comfort. Did she deserve comfort now?

Her baby boy was once as sweet as the baby they were singing about. She could almost feel him sleeping in her arms, his warmth melting her frozen heart. She felt as one with this Mary that they sang of: the questions she must have had, and the ponderings in her heart. Did the other Mary experience the soul-searing pain she did? The pain that never leaves, but cuts a new jagged edge each day? Mary believed she did. Yet the song spoke of purpose, reaching beyond Mary's own dreams for her baby boy into a far deeper and higher destiny.

The song ended. The carollers stood still. A long, quiet pause filled the room. All eyes were on her. Suddenly Mary was aware of tears streaming down her face. She took a small step forward.

"Thank you. That is a beautiful song. You'll never know… my Luke… he knew Mary's boy. He's with Him now."

Still they all watched her. Were they afraid her sudden rush of openness was cause for concern for her emotional health? Mary swiped at her tears and attempted a reassuring smile.

"Would you like to stay for coffee?"

It was all the invitation needed as the carollers swarmed into the living room. Al smiled at her and shook her hand as if they'd just met. Mary laughed. She almost felt like a new person. She suddenly yearned to know more about what Luke had known, about Mary's boy. There was so much she didn't know.

*Written by Mark Lowry and Buddy Greene; published 1991.

Christmas Whiskers
by

L.L. MacLellan

Quiet and still, the forest slumbered comfortably, its floor covered by a diamond-encrusted blanket of powdery snow. Two lone figures trudged slowly along, pausing every so often to tie up a stray boot lace or to inspect a set of rabbit tracks that crossed their path. The child, a little girl perhaps three or four years old, was bundled against the cold, and rendered nearly immobile by her many layers of protective winter clothing. Only her ruddy cheeks and bright eyes could be seen, sparkling from beneath a red, hand-knitted toque. Her small, mittened hand was engulfed in her father's larger one, and their slow footsteps left a haphazard trail in the newly fallen snow. Christmas snow. Huge flakes swirled around them, falling in slow motion, and the child reached out and caught one. She stood and studied it a moment, admiring its crisp, fragile beauty. She held it up for her father to see.

"I tot a snowflake, Papa. Look! It's so pretty."

Papa bent down for a closer look. "It is pretty, Sweetheart. And unique. There isn't another one like it." Just then a fat, fluffy flake landed gently on the tip of her nose and they laughed at this together, his eyes twinkling into hers. Straightening, he glanced around. Their home was just up ahead, around a bend in the trail, but they had been out for a while and he could tell her little legs were tiring. "Would you like a ride, Little One?"

His daughter held out her arms in answer and he swooped her up, snuggling her close for a moment before swinging her around onto his broad shoulders. The little girl giggled and reached down to brush her mitten across her father's cheek.

"Your whiskers tickled me when you picked me up, Papa."

He chuckled and ran a gloved hand over his chin. "Don't you like my Christmas whiskers?"

"Well…" She hesitated, torn between honesty and kindness. "They tickle too much."

He laughed at her answer. "That's what Mama says too. That's why I only grow them at Christmas time. I'll shave them off when the holidays are over, and then they won't tickle you again until next Christmas." Papa turned. "We'd better head back home. Christmas dinner is almost ready. I think I can smell the turkey."

The little girl sniffed the air loudly. "Mmm! I can too! And pumpkin pie. And olives!"

"Olives? You can smell the olives?"

"Mm-hmm," she mumbled, her face now buried in the scratchy warmth of her father's wool hat.

Now Papa sniffed. "Well, whatever it is, it smells good to me. Let's hurry!" He quickened his pace, joggling along so that his daughter had to cling on tightly. Father and daughter arrived home, warm and laughing, and brushed the Christmas snow from their clothes.

Less than two weeks later Papa was gone, snatched away from them when his car slid out of control on an icy road and into an oncoming truck. The girl stood at the front door beside her mother when the pastor's wife came with the policeman. Their little house filled with bouquets of hothouse flowers and potted chrysanthemums, and their country church filled with grieving family and friends for the funeral. Everyone was immensely kind, offering sympathy and support, but life was never again the same.

Time passed, the little girl grew up, and even though she had never really known her father, she missed him all her life. Eventually she met a very kind, very special man whose eyes twinkled into hers when he smiled at her, and one warm autumn day they were married. Before long they had a baby, a little girl, and life became very busy. Memories of her childhood, of her father, grew dim, obscured by the hustle and bustle of everyday life.

One winter morning the very kind, very special man came to the breakfast table and leaned over to give his wife a kiss. "Merry Christmas, Sweetheart," he said. "What do you think of my new look?" His wife studied the carefully trimmed stubble on his chin with a gentle smile. Christmas whiskers. Faded memories stirred slowly, then came flooding back: memories of Papa, of their last walk together, and of Papa's Christmas whiskers. Wordlessly, she reached out a hand and trailed her fingers slowly down her husband's cheek.

"Me do it! Me do it, too!" insisted their daughter.

They laughed at her imperious nature. "Sure, honey. Come here." The tiny girl stepped close and reached up little fingers to touch the unfamiliar whiskers.

"It's pokey," she announced, wriggling her nose.

"Pokey? I thought it was distinguished," her father protested, laughing. He grabbed his daughter close and nuzzled her neck gently, causing the little girl to shriek with laughter. Glancing up, he caught his wife's tender gaze, her eyes misted with happy tears.

"Is anything wrong?" he asked quietly.

"No," she said softly. She looked at the two of them, father and daughter, together, their faces radiant with joy. "No, my love," she said. "Everything is just right."

On the Eve

by

Marcia Lee Laycock

How foolish I was. I hadn't even bothered to check the weather in Whitehorse before flying out of Vancouver. The plane was able to land, but by the next morning the temperature had plummeted and my flight to Dawson City was cancelled.

"But I have to get to Dawson in time for Christmas." I plunked my cat cage on the counter. Kitty stood up, meowed, and stretched.

The airline attendant shrugged. "Planes don't fly when it's this cold," he said. "You could rent a car." He scanned my West Coast clothing, his eyes lingering on my high heels before adding, "If you have the right gear."

"The right gear?"

"It's over five hundred kilometres of rough road to Dawson. You'll need warm clothing and emergency gear, like candles and a down sleeping bag."

I sighed and scratched Kitty's ear with one finger through the wire cage. "I have to get there," I said. The attendant pointed me to the car rental booth and soon I was on my way.

The rental agent had suggested I stop and buy a down coat and boots. "Mukluks are the best," she said. As I pulled out of the parking lot I thought about it—for about two seconds. But the shops would be crazy busy on the day before Christmas. It would take too much time, and money I couldn't spare. I had to be with my husband on Christmas Eve, even if I had to risk driving five hundred kilometres of rough road without all the special gear. The car's heater was blasting heat around me, and Kitty was like a little furnace. She'd keep me warm.

There weren't many vehicles on the road once I got past the outskirts of the city. The temperature on the dash read minus sixty-five. Could it really be that cold? I switched the heater to defrost but it was barely keeping a small hat-shaped spot on the windshield clear. When I turned the car north towards Dawson, I experienced another moment of hesitation. But I couldn't wait to see the look on Davy's face when he saw me at his door.

The car, which had been showing definite signs of exhaustion, chugged a few times before it died. I pulled Kitty out of her cage and tucked her under my jacket, keeping my hands wrapped around her tiny body for warmth.

Someone would come along soon, I thought, trying to calculate how far I was from the last house I'd seen.

It didn't take long for the windshield to completely frost over. I couldn't stop shivering and soon I couldn't feel my toes. As I tucked my chin deeper into the front of my thin coat, I realized even a small candle would have helped. I wished I'd taken the time to buy that down coat and boots and mittens. But it was too late for wishes.

Funny what you think about when you believe you're going to die. I worried that Kitty would freeze to death too. I worried about how I'd look when Davy saw my frozen face. And then I started thinking about something he'd said the last time we'd been together. He'd been talking about becoming a Christian, something that had just happened to him.

"It's almost Christmas, Lucy," he'd said. "Do you know what it's really all about?"

I didn't answer then but I started to think about it now. I remembered Davy's smile as he said all you had to do was ask Jesus to help you and He'd send His angels.

"That's how much He loves you, Lucy," he'd said.

"He'll send angels, just like the ones who appeared to the shepherds in Bethlehem."

So I asked.

It didn't take long for my head to start nodding. It would be so nice to sleep, just drift off for a while. I'd been dreaming about those angels, hearing the rush of their wings and the trumpet-like sound of their voices. So when the glow of lights made the windshield sparkle, I thought I was imagining it. When two guys in funny looking hats knocked on my window I thought I was hallucinating. I couldn't move my arm enough to open the door. When they got it open, I couldn't move my legs so they lifted Kitty and me out and into their truck, and got us to a nearby house where they gave me hot soup and promised they'd get me to Dawson in the morning.

Funny. Those guys didn't look like angels, but I fell asleep thinking about that night in Bethlehem.

Jenny's Christmas Eve Homecoming

by Gladys Krueger

"Did she say for sure she's coming?" Henry looked up from his book as his wife, Helen, peered out the window.

"No. But it's Christmas Eve. Jenny hasn't been here for such a long time and I invited her a whole month ago to come for Christmas."

Helen looked over at the table set for three. Her gift for Jenny was wrapped and placed beside her plate. Christmas napkins and candles added a festive look to the table. The aroma of turkey, vegetables, and pie filled the kitchen. Helen looked out the window again. "I think I see her headlights turning in," she said happily, and checked again that all was ready. "She said she couldn't stay long if she came," she added.

Helen flung the door open before Jenny could knock. "I'm so glad you made it," she beamed. Jenny deftly stooped to take off her boots before Helen could give the welcoming hug.

Henry looked up and said, "Merry Christmas, Peanut," his term of endearment when she was young.

"Oh, Dad. I'm past the 'Peanut' stage now," she chided. "But Merry Christmas to you, too." She added, "Mmm. The turkey smells good. Is it a range bird?"

"No," Helen replied with some misgiving. "We couldn't afford the range birds and this one looked real fine." *It is so hard to cook for Jenny since she has become so careful about her food.*

"Well. I guess it won't kill me this once," Jenny

30

replied. "Let's eat. I'm so hungry I could eat anything!"

They sat at the table. Henry thanked the Lord for the food, the year, and Jenny's safe arrival.

"It's wonderful to have you here with us again," Helen said warmly.

"Well, I can't stay long, but I thought I'd better come or you'd be mad at me."

Helen flinched. "Jenny—when have I been mad at you?"

"Things change," Jenny laughed as she checked the brussels sprouts. "I guess there's no use asking if these are organic. You really are going to have to change your eating habits," she added before Helen could respond.

"What's this?" Jenny picked up the gift near her plate. "I thought we didn't do presents anymore."

"It caught my eye when I saw it in the store," Helen said tentatively. "I thought you'd like it. Why don't you open it?"

"I'll open it when we finish dinner. So, how are you both keeping? Hey, Dad, what's with the cane by your chair?"

"Just getting older," Henry smiled. "I feel safe with it. The cane helps me keep my balance."

"Whatever works," Jenny said flippantly.

After they finished the main course, Helen got up to brew the coffee and cut the pie.

"Guess I have time to open this now." Jenny picked up the gift Helen had chosen and wrapped so carefully. "I'd better see what Mom thought I might still like."

She ripped the papers off and looked at the delicate bracelet sitting in a satin-lined box. "Nice colour. Thanks Mom." She set it aside. "What kind of pie did you make?"

"Your favourite—at least it used to be," Helen said quietly. "It's pumpkin with whipped cream."

"Oh. Skip the cream, Mom. You know how fattening that is. But I'll have the pie. Did you know I've learned that pumpkin is actually good for you? I hope you don't mind if I leave the crust and just eat the filling."

"Sure. Do you still drink coffee?"

"Pour me a cup and make it black." Jenny sighed and looked at her watch.

"So," Henry said. "I guess you're pretty busy. What are you doing these days?"

"Busy is right!" she replied. "What are you up to now that you are retired?" Jenny asked, avoiding her Dad's question. "Busy, too, I'll bet," she answered for him. Then she added, "Good pie, Mom. You're a good cook. Just watch the calories and go organic. Well, it's good to see you both, but time's a-wasting. I'd better go. The weather could change tonight." Jenny got up and headed for her coat.

"Don't forget your gift," Helen reminded her.

"Oh yeah. I can't forget that, can I?"

Within minutes the door shut and she was gone. Helen looked wearily at the table. Henry offered to help clean up.

"Let's just sit a few minutes and have another cup of coffee," she said.

Henry poured the coffee and gave her a kiss as he set it in front of her. "Let's sit on the sofa in front of the fireplace."

"You know what I'm thinking?" Helen asked after they settled comfortably.

"You always amaze me. What are you thinking now?" Henry asked as he put his arm around her shoulder.

"I'm thinking that we just experienced the first Christmas. Love and a gift given with no sign of apprecia-tion—isn't that God leaving Heaven to be born in a manger? And with the God of Heaven we pray that one day our girl will really come home."

"Amen to that." Henry nodded and sipped his coffee.

"I'll always tell you what I'm thinking even if you don't ask." Helen paused and looked at him quizzically. "So what's going on in your head?"

"I'm thinking how much I love you and your non-organic cooking!"

They both smiled as she snuggled against him. "The dishes can wait."

The Parcel

by

Wendy L. Macdonald

"Ouch!"

Jaylinn shifted her groceries to one side and looked down to discover she'd stubbed her toe on a brown parcel leaning against her porch door. The mystery package was the size of a box of oranges.

Who could it be from?

She set the bags on the oak bench, flicked on the Christmas lights, and then picked up the package. It was heavier than she expected it to be, and it was addressed to her, but she didn't recognize the tidy handwriting or the sender's name. Her spirit sagged as she remembered this would be her first December not receiving a box of goodies from her mother.

I wish I could have gone home last year—but how was I to know it would be her last Christmas? And there's no way I could have driven through that record-breaking snowstorm.

Her mother's heart attack last spring had come without warning and stolen without mercy. But God had shown grace in allowing it to happen while her mother had friends over for Bible study. She was grateful her mom hadn't died alone. And those same ladies had been a comfort as she fumbled her way through the funeral arrangements. *Lord, You're here with me, and I trust You'll comfort me now too.*

The sound of a vehicle driving up startled her.

Oh dear, I'd hoped to get the lasagna into the oven

33

before Tanya got here.

Her best friend waved as she closed her car door behind her. "I hope I'm not too early. I brought a salad—and dessert. You'll never guess what I made."

"You didn't."

Tanya opened the passenger door and hauled out a large wicker basket covered with a linen tablecloth. "Yup. And don't be counting calories. You're the skinniest person I know."

"What would I do without you?"

"Thought we'd drown our sorrows in chocolate." Tanya bumped the car door closed with her generous hip and made her way to the porch, crunching through the snow as she added more footprints to the snow-covered sidewalk.

Jaylinn gasped. "Be careful not to slip! I'm way behind schedule and haven't had time to shovel since two snowfalls ago. Good thing it's lighter than …" her voice broke, "than … last year's."

Jaylinn bit her lip to hold back tears that begged to flow as she tried not to think of her mother's snowbound Christmas last year—alone.

Tanya set her basket on the porch floor beside a wicker chair. "I bet you need a hug."

"Sure do."

They embraced, and Jaylinn enjoyed the fragrance of lavender emanating from Tanya's wool scarf, reminding her of her mother's garden.

They carted their treasures to the warm and welcoming kitchen that glowed with Christmas lights around each window.

Tanya pointed to the parcel. "Who's it from? Are you going to open it?"

"I don't know who it's from."

Tanya crossed her arms. "All the more reason to unwrap it."

Jaylinn grabbed a pair of scissors and removed the

brown paper. Inside she found an orange box filled with a sparkling menagerie of giftwrapped items. A red envelope, addressed to her, crowned a stack of old letters tied together with a red ribbon. She slipped it out from the rest, tore it open, and read the beautifully handwritten words:

> *Dear Jaylinn,*
> *Your mother and I exchanged a lot of letters over the years. I thought you'd enjoy reading these. She often wrote about you. I've added some homemade jams and other small gifts.*
>
> *Merry Christmas in Christ,*
>
> *Mabel Bennett*

Tears blurred Jaylinn's eyes, but she wiped them away, not wanting to spoil the visit.

Tanya touched her shoulder. "What does it say?"

Too overwhelmed by a mixture of grief and joy to speak, Jaylinn handed the letter to her friend.

Tanya read it and shook her head. "Wow! I prayed God would send something extra special to comfort you."

Jaylinn grabbed a tissue from her pocket and dabbed the corners of her eyes. "Now I have two gifts to thank God for."

Tanya tilted her head to one side. "Huh?"

"Your company for Christmas, dear friend. You didn't think I meant the chocolate—did you?"

Hope for Jimmy
by
Ruth L. Snyder

Even under two blankets, four-year-old Jimmy lay shivering. It had to be the coldest night of the year. Then again, any night was cold during winter out on the streets. He rolled over and felt a sharp poke in his hip from a pebble under his cardboard bed. Although his teeth chattered, he was happy. *I'm dry. I ate today. Momma will be back soon, and I'm safe.*

He peered into the darkness and listened intently as footsteps drew closer. "Jimmy, it's Momma." He sighed with relief. It was scary when she was away. What would happen if she didn't come back? Who would take care of him? How would he find food? He snuggled back into his blankets and closed his eyes. He was tired. Now that Momma was back he could relax.

***

"Jimmy, wake up!" Momma shook him. "You need to get up."

Jimmy's tummy rumbled. He rubbed his eyes and sat up. The sun was peeking over the horizon. He stood quickly, stomping his feet while folding his blankets. Momma folded the cardboard. They stashed their makeshift home and blankets behind a nearby dumpster.

"Thanks for your help, Jimmy. You're a good boy." Momma smiled at him.

He returned the smile. "What are we doing today?"

36

"I'm taking you to a centre. They'll take care of you and feed you while I go to some job interviews."

Jimmy looked down at his boots. The smile slipped off his face. "Can't I come too?"

"I'm sorry, son, but people don't take kindly to kids tagging along for job interviews. Remember, I need a job so I can earn money to buy the things we need."

He nodded his head slowly. He did not want to sleep on the street forever. Maybe if Momma had a job they could live in a real house. Maybe he could even have a dog for a pet. He bit his lip. He would be brave. Just for his Momma. He wanted her to be proud of him.

"Ready?"

He nodded and placed his small hand into hers. He could see his breath as they walked, but his body felt warmer now that they were moving. As their boots crunched in the snow, Jimmy heard music. The words said something about a manger for a bed.

"What's a manger?"

Momma looked puzzled.

"That music. It said something about a manger for a bed."

"Oh. That." She looked sad. "Some people say that baby Jesus's mother put him to bed in hay, in a cow's trough."

Jimmy wondered if that would be warmer to sleep in than his cardboard bed. "Momma, what does that sign say?"

She paused. "So many questions." Her eyes twinkled. "It says, 'No Parking. Shipping and Receiving.'"

Jimmy wrinkled his face. "What's that mean?"

Momma started walking again. "That's where big trucks pick up and drop off things."

"Someday I'll drive one of those trucks."

"Maybe. Now hurry. We're almost there."

A few minutes later, he and Momma walked

through a door into a building. It was as warm as a summer day with the sun shining on his face. Momma talked to two ladies. Then a door opened and he saw some children playing with toys.

"Hi Jimmy. My name is Marta. I'll be looking after you until your Mom gets back, okay?"

He gazed into her chocolate brown eyes. She looked kind, and her voice was gentle. Jimmy nodded and waved to Momma as she walked away.

"Here's a train. Do you want me to help you set up the track?"

Jimmy shook his head no. He wanted to check out all the other people before he played. He had to make sure this was a safe place. He counted, something Momma had taught him. One, two, three, four, five, six. There were six other kids and the lady. What was her name again? Oh yes, Marta. All of the kids were playing. The lady was doing something with food.

"Children, it's time for a snack. Please wash your hands and find a seat at the table." Jimmy followed the other children. He wished he could wash his whole body in the warm water. The soap smelled like flowers. Pretty like Momma.

Marta talked to them as they were eating bananas, oranges, cheese, and crackers. "This afternoon we have a special Christmas party. You'll have lots of fun playing games and eating food. Your parents will pick you up after the party is over."

The day passed quickly for Jimmy. He was safe. He was warm. And he had food to eat. It was wonderful just to have toys to play with again. He hoped Momma was having as much fun as he was.

"It's time to go to the party, children." Marta opened the door and led the children down some stairs to a huge room.

Jimmy looked around the room and smiled. The

whole room seemed to sparkle. There was a huge green tree with glittering decorations and beautiful twinkling lights. There were tables set up around the room. The lady said they could pick what they wanted to do. He chose a table piled high with shortbread cookies. They smelled yummy, like the bread place he walked by with Momma. He did his best as he put red and green icing onto a tree-shaped cookie. Other children around the table were eating their cookies, but he asked if he could wrap his for later. He wanted to surprise Momma and give her the cookie for dessert that night.

He followed the other children to a table with pictures and words. He knew Momma would be happy to receive a card, especially if he made it. He picked a purple one. Purple was her favourite colour. He looked through the pictures. Oh, there was one with a baby in some hay in a wooden thing. He tapped a lady on the arm. "Is this what they call a manger?"

She looked at the picture. "Yes, it is."

"Why did his mother put him there? Didn't she love him?"

"She loved him just as much as your mom loves you. His parents were poor and they were travelling when Jesus was born. The only place that had any room for them was a building where animals lived."

"So his mom did the bestest she could. Didn't she?"

Other children around the table nodded. Jimmy decided he needed to ask Momma more about this story later.

When they were finished, Marta stood up. "We hope you've had fun this afternoon. There are snacks for all of you, but first we want to give each of you a gift."

Shiny bows decorated the tops of a mountain of packages. One by one the children were called to receive a gift. When Jimmy's name was called, he went and took a large rectangular package out of Marta's hands. "Thanks," he said.

She smiled back at him. "You're very welcome,

Jimmy. I'm glad you could come today. Merry Christmas!"

He had to slow his feet down as he returned to the table. He grinned when he saw Momma there waiting. She smiled. "Are you going to open it, Jimmy?"

He nodded and ripped the paper off. He whooped when he saw the red truck in the box. "See, I told you I'd be a delivery truck driver!"

Momma chuckled. "Yes, you did. I think you're right. And it looks like I'm going to be a waitress, starting tomorrow."

He looked up. Her eyes were sparkling. Jimmy grinned and gave her a big hug. "Way to go, Momma." He took the cookie and card out of his pocket and handed them to her. "I was going to give these to you later, but I can't wait. Today's a day to celebrate, don't you think?"

Home for Christmas
by
Carol Elaine Harrison

Christmas lights illuminating the porch and a lit-up tree in the front window beckoned Katie as she dashed up the steps to her Gramma's house. After her long day at work, and then fending off the unwanted advances of a drunken colleague at her office Christmas party, her preference would have been to go back to her own apartment and curl up on her leather sofa. But a little voice in her head hounded her with the words, *Go see Gramma—now!*

She shook her head as if to free her mind from all these thoughts and knocked before trying the door handle. It moved at her touch. She entered the house that had been home for most of her life.

"Gramma, I'm home."

Katie dropped her bag, threw her jacket towards the hooks by the door and rushed to the living room when Gramma did not answer her call. She spied her grandmother in her favourite chair, with her Bible open on her lap; head drooped in sleep or maybe prayer.

Katie dropped to her knees and touched Gramma's hand, hoping not to startle her. No response. She felt for a pulse and found none. She tried again with the same result. "Gramma, no! Don't go! I need you."

Choking back sobs, she phoned 9-1-1. While waiting for help to arrive she knew two things with sudden clarity. Her grandmother now resided in the Heaven she had spoken of frequently. And secondly, all the things Katie had run towards in the big city—her glamorous, professionally decorated apartment, her great job, and the multitude of entertainment choices—never filled the spot this grandmother, who raised her, had always fulfilled. Katie realized how much she had missed the stability, traditions, and love she had grown up with. Why did it take her until now to recognize it?

The next few days passed in a blur of activity. Neighbours and church people dropped by with food, offers to help, and fond memories of Gramma. However, when Katie returned to work, her boss was not sympathetic of her request for more time off, and none of her colleagues called to offer their condolences. The sharp contrast pricked her heart. She began to question her perception of church attendance being too old fashioned, and her choice not to visit Gramma in person more often. The pastor's words of hope at the funeral flooded her mind with memories of Bible lessons learned in Sunday school, church sermons, and from her Gramma.

On Christmas Eve, Katie curled up on the familiar old sofa at her Gramma's house to open an envelope she had discovered while sorting through the papers on the old roll-top desk. Her name, in Gramma's delicate handwriting, graced the envelope. She pulled out a single sheet of paper.

December 15

Dear Katie,
By the time you read this letter, I'll be home with Jesus. I have prayed for you every day. I long for you to remember the babe in the manger who became the Christ of the cross; giving His life so you can be His child. He loves you and is waiting for you with open arms. My heart's desire is to see you again—in Heaven. Never forget how much I have loved you.

Love,
Gramma.

Tears fell on the paper as Katie begged God's forgiveness for running away from Him. Peace enveloped her and she heard God's voice whisper *Welcome home, My child.*

An Unexpected Gift
by

Nina Faye Morey

There it is! It's perfect! Geneva couldn't believe her eyes. She'd searched the shops and boutiques for several days in vain. Now here she was at the airport, about to fly home for Christmas, and she'd unexpectedly found it in the gift shop's window. A beautiful sapphire blue shawl draped over a female mannequin. It was the perfect present for her mom.

Geneva hurried across the aisle towards the shop, hauling her carry-on roughshod over the tile floor. She had only ten minutes before she was to meet her sister in the airport's coffee shop.

A lovely lavender scent greeted Geneva as she entered the gift shop, and she drew in a deep, relaxing breath. She discovered the fragrance was coming from a small humidifier on the cashier's counter. Glancing around, she saw that amidst all the usual gift shop merchandise were scores of captivating scarves, shawls, and cashmere sweaters draped over dowels, folded neatly on glass shelving, and hanging from circular chrome racks. A small display counter housed dazzling crystal and gem-stone earrings, necklaces, and bracelets.

An exotic, dark-complexioned sales lady popped up from behind the jewelry counter. "May I help you?" she asked with a delightful accent that Geneva couldn't quite place.

"Oh yes, please. You have a beautiful blue shawl in

43

your window that I'd like to buy."

"Certainly," the sales lady said, already moving gracefully towards the mannequin in the window. She gently removed the shawl and held it out to drape around Geneva's shoulders. "Try it on, dear, and have a look in the mirror." She nodded towards a vintage full-length mirror standing in the corner. "You'll see how beautifully it drapes over your shoulders."

Geneva was already sold on the shawl, but she couldn't resist trying it on. The colour would accent the deep blue of her mother's eyes, and the cozy fabric would keep her toasty warm. Her mom had been confined to a wheelchair since a car accident a couple of years ago and always complained of feeling chilly in the drafty hallways of her nursing home.

The sales lady slipped the shawl around Geneva's shoulders, and they admired it in the mirror. It did indeed drape beautifully. A delicate floral pattern outlined with fine silver thread and an intricately knotted fringe gave the shawl a luxurious look. She stroked it, and the fine Pashmina wool fabric felt exquisitely soft under her fingertips.

"Yes, it's perfect," Geneva nodded. "I'll take it." She removed the shawl from her shoulders and handed it back to the sales lady, who carefully folded it as she glided towards the sales counter. She proceeded to delicately wrap the shawl in layers of white tissue paper, ensuring the fringe was tucked in neatly before placing it inside a lovely lavender bag with the name of the shop printed in silver lettering. *Classy!* Geneva felt pleasantly pampered.

She rummaged through her oversized handbag in search of her wallet. Extracting her credit card, Geneva completed the transaction and tucked the exquisite parcel safely away in an outside pocket of her carry-on. Thanking the elegant saleslady, she hurried from the gift shop.

Geneva glanced at her watch. Her sister was probably already waiting for her in the coffee shop. You could always count on Jill to be on time.

Geneva hadn't seen her older sister in over five years and wasn't sure what to expect. The last time had been at the funeral for Jill's husband. Sadly, he'd died from cancer in his early fifties. They'd only talked a few times on the phone since then and exchanged birthday and Christmas cards. They'd always had an uneasy relationship, but they'd drifted even further apart over the years. Although Geneva had made some attempts to get together, her sister hadn't seemed receptive. In fact, she'd been surprised when Jill had called a week ago to say that she was flying to visit her daughter in Vancouver over Christmas and would love to meet Geneva for coffee during her brief layover at the local airport. Geneva told her that, by coincidence, she'd already be there to catch a flight to visit their mother, and she'd be delighted to meet with her. Now, as she turned into the corridor leading to the coffee shop, she said a quick, silent prayer: *Lord, help me to do and say the right things to restore my relationship with my sister and bring us into a new season of love and grace. Amen.*

Geneva entered the coffee shop and glanced around nervously in search of her sister. She wasn't sure she'd even recognize Jill since she had a habit of changing the style and colour of her hair and eyeglasses every couple of years. But as soon as she entered, Jill raised her hand and waved her over to a table tucked into a quiet corner at the back of the coffee shop. Geneva hurried over and Jill rose to greet her. As they embraced, Geneva began to feel a bit more relaxed.

"How are you, Jill?" she asked as she settled herself at the tiny table across from her sister. She noted that Jill's hair was shorter and a different shade of blonde, and she was wearing new glasses with a bright frame that complemented the colour of her eyes. "You look wonderful!" she commented with genuine admiration.

"Thanks, Geneva. You look lovely yourself. I see you're wearing glasses now, too."

Geneva chuckled. "Yes, my eyesight's not what it used to be. I guess I can't tease you about being four-eyes anymore." She cringed inside, immediately regretting her careless comment. Somehow she always managed to say the wrong thing whenever she was nervous. They'd experienced their share of sibling rivalry through the years, but she hoped all that was behind them now. She definitely hadn't intended to start their conversation off on a sour note.

Jill seemed unperturbed. "I'd forgotten about that," she said, a smile tugging at the edges of her expertly lined lips.

"I love that shade of blonde on you," Geneva ventured, trying to make amends for the verbal gaffe. She still marvelled at her older sister's sense of style. While she was the introverted bookworm with the casual wardrobe and no makeup, Jill was the extroverted fashionista.

"Thanks, Geneva. I've received a lot of compliments on it."

They both ordered coffee and pie à la mode and spent the next half hour catching up on all the news about their children and reminiscing about their younger days. Geneva was surprised to discover that her sister's demeanour had changed. She wondered if it could be related to Jill's loss of her husband. She found herself actually feeling quite comfortable and enjoying her sister's company. It seemed that their old rivalries, grudges, and competitiveness had faded into the background. Geneva found herself sharing little morsels of her life with her sister that she never dreamed she would.

Their easy conversation seemed to smooth out the

rough edges of their normally rocky relationship. Feeling uncharacteristically gregarious, Geneva felt a sudden urge to share her recent shopping feat with her sister. She began explaining how she'd spent hours looking for just the right Christmas gifts for her loved ones this year, but had trouble finding that last perfect present.

"Oh, I know just what you mean," Jill interjected. "It's so hard sometimes to know what to get for someone." She had retrieved her shoulder bag from the chair beside her and was rooting through it for something, apparently unsure of which pocket she'd put it in. Then with a triumphant smile, she extracted a small gift-wrapped box and handed it to Geneva. "Merry Christmas, Geneva, I hope you like it."

Geneva looked at the tiny gift box in astonishment. It took her a few seconds to regain her composure. She hadn't expected this. With shaky fingers, she untied the neat little bow and tore away the wrapping paper that concealed a small jewel box with the monogram of a designer jeweller. She gently opened it to reveal a stunning pair of earrings with pearls set in gold. It took her a moment to find her voice. "Oh, Jill, you remembered my birthstone! They're beautiful! Thank you."

Jill was beaming. "I'm so glad you like them, Geneva. It's been so many years since we've exchanged Christmas gifts, and I really wanted to give you something special."

Geneva was filled with a strange mixture of joy and remorse. Despite her deep desire to reconcile their relationship, it hadn't occurred to her to add her sister's name to her Christmas list, even when she knew they'd be seeing each other. Her cheeks flushed with shame. Suddenly, she had an inspiration. She bent down and unzipped the top pocket of her carry-on and removed her precious parcel. "Here's your gift, Jill," she said, setting the lavender bag down on the table in front of her sister.

Jill tenderly pulled the layers of tissue paper from the bag and began slowly unwrapping her present. She stared at the exquisite blue shawl for a moment and then lovingly stroked the soft Pashmina fabric. She was uncharacteristically silent for several seconds. When she finally lifted her eyes to meet Geneva's gaze, they glistened brightly under the harsh lighting. "It's lovely," she said softly. "Your gifts are always so thoughtful, Geneva. Thank you."

"You're, welcome, Jill." Geneva watched her sister gracefully drape the shawl over the shoulders of her winter white jacket. It looked fabulous on her. *Of course! The Pashmina's a perfect present for Jill, too. Her eyes are the same deep shade of blue as Mom's. I'll find another shawl for Mom. I know she has always wanted her two daughters to have a closer relationship. If she were here, I don't think she'd begrudge me giving this one to Jill instead of her.*

Geneva's initial shame over her faux pas had transformed into elation. Although she'd purchased the shawl for her mother, giving it to her sister had turned their visit into a joyful occasion that would be etched in her memory forever. *Thank You, Lord, for answering my prayer.*

Sense of Value
by
Ruth Smith Meyer

Little babe
newly birthed, leaving glories of heaven—
    golden streets
        gem laden walls
            divine scents
                healing aromas
    —beyond the grasp of mortal minds.

To arrive
in a dark, humid, crude stable—
    no golden streets
        no gem laden walls
            but dank scents
                animal aromas
    —lowly place for even human birth.

Come wise men
in royal robes from lands afar, bringing their best—
    shining gold
        sweet frankincense
            fragrant myrrh
                rich treasures
    —to express their hearts' devotion.

Like children,
who gather bright yellow dandelions—
    clutching proud
        impressive gifts
            hearts full
                overflowing devotion
    —present them to their mothers.

While human
side of the babe looked on in delight—
    the divine
        must have winked at
            commonplace
                earthly offerings
    —but he knew their hearts' intent and tenderly smiled.

So It Was Thought
by
Alvin Ens

"He was the son, so it was thought, of Joseph" (Luke 3:23).

after 30 years so it was thought
so it was thought—
though local gossip prattled that it was an illegitimate birth
though his proclamations confounded the teachers
though his miracles astonished the crowds
it was thought that his origins were human

did the shepherds who told everyone
go back to their sheep and let rumour remain
did the magi become secretive and quiet
did Zechariah and John not preach prophetic fulfillment
did time dull the brains of relatives and friends
so they let it be thought

the thinking crowd is unresponsive—
it is a logical expression or so it was thought
that Jesus was the son of Joseph
forget the divine
we do so every Christmas
forget the divine in the sweet story of birth

Advent Song

by

Katherine Kavanagh Hoffman

We await his coming.
King of the universe born in a stable
God of creation sleeps in a manger
Rough and crude
Hard and cold.

We await his coming.
Young Mary holds him wrapped in coarse swaddling
Joseph stands over him guarding his family
Awestruck
Confused.

We await his coming.
Shepherds come running filled with strange stories
Hearts beating wildly breathless from haste
Wide eyed
With hope.

We await his coming.

Sound the Joy
by
Connie Mae Inglis

The broken world in solemn stillness lay,
Year after year of prophet-proclaimed
Silence.
Hopelessness heaped upon
Heavy hearts:
Royally,
   Politically,
      Religiously,
         Personally.
Joy-less suffering.

Time ripens—
   Shifts.
"See, I am doing a new thing!
Now it springs up;
Do you not perceive it?"*

Silent skies awaken with peaceful wings unfurled,
Appearance after appearance preparing—promising
Good news.
Spirit of hope filling up
Faithful servants:
Zechariah,
   Mary,
      Elizabeth,
         Joseph.
Joy-supreme celebration.

Repeat the sounding joy,

   Sounding joy,

JOY!

Isaiah 43:19

Holy Day
by
Katherine Kavanagh Hoffman

This is one of the holy days
when heaven kissed earth and changed it forever
leaving a touch, a taste of eternity
working its way into the fabric of a world fallen.

There is an imprint now, begun with the baby in the manger.
Everything is altered from the inside out.

Slowly, slowly
creation is restored
and the hearts of humankind are mended.

So turn to that child with wonder that God has come among us
to heal us in every way
to heal all of creation.

This is one of the holy days.

Let's Not Forget

by

Patricia A. Earl

Christmas time has come once more,
hear it knocking at your door;
time for friends to reconnect,
are you busy? I suspect
much to do, so little time,
gone the silence and sublime;
shopping, baking, deck the tree,
cleaning, wrapping--can it be
lost amid the to and fro
God's special gift to earth below?

The Christ of Christmas came to give
peace and joy to all who live,
to all who would believe, submit
to truths within the Holy Writ;
this costly gift from God above
expression of His selfless love.

Amidst the running to and fro,
the ads, the voices saying, "Go!"
let's not forget the reason why
we celebrate, and let us try
to slow our pace, to stop and pray
to thank the Father every day
for Jesus Christ our Lord and King
and with the angels let us sing,
"Hallelujah to the One
who gave to us, His precious Son!"

Waiting

by

Donna Gartshore

The night sky stark and lonely
uninterrupted by stars. A lamb bawls and sniffs the air for
its mother. Shepherds, bored, think of home,
wives with the sustenance of steaming stews,
beds for the bone-weary.

They think they are only waiting for
the night to end. They don't know
they are waiting for
the sky to explode with light
for lives to be changed forever.

Waiting for the traffic light to change,
Honking horns,
Starlight dimmed, overshadowed
by artificial orbs of light.
Waiting for supper, for movement,
for retirement, for the next big thing.

We've forgotten that night
the sky exploded with God's promise
and lives were changed forever.

In a stable, a teenage mother's hand
cups the face of her newborn son,
with gentleness and reverence.
She waits for what comes next.

Waiting for deliverance.

A grandmother's gnarled hand caresses the face
of a grandchild whose name she can't
remember. But his smile comforts her as
others buzz around
waiting for deliveries, waiting for music
waiting for presents.
She waits and wonders if what comes next
is an end or a beginning.
And she remembers stories
of shepherds and skies
exploding with light
and the meek, life-changing cry
of an infant king.

Waiting,
Two thousand years and more
Shepherds' and angels' proclamations.

Babies cry and mothers sing songs of comfort
and ponder things in their hearts.
Weary workers return home craving
sustenance and rest.
Families gather and laugh
and eat and weep
and wait.
Life changes so much and yet
not at all.

Remember we are all still waiting.
Remember Who we
are waiting for.

Early Visitors

by

Alvin Ens

"When they had seen him,
they spread the word" (Luke 2:17).

Dusty, dirty, smelly, unschooled shepherds
sleeping in the fields rain or shine
with sheep's poo on their sandals
to them was entrusted God's message
leaving all, they came with haste to see
and after they had seen, they spread the word

Not like the eastern magi, schooled philosophers
travelling in concert in convoy, with gifts and plenty
seeking a king in the capital city, asking a hostile governor
they worship and present gifts
then go home a different route

Anticipation
by
Ruth A.M. Sakstad

A virgin has conceived
Not of man's designs
Through the Holy Spirit's working
In accordance with God's will
Christ Child has come
Incarnate God
Providing salvation to the world
Angels heralded His coming
The shepherds came to worship Him
Immanuel, God with us
Offerings from the Magi fit for King and Saviour
Now let us come, adore Christ the Lord

Our Christmas Gifts

by

Elaine Ingalls Hogg

As we make our plans this Christmas,
Where we'll worship the birth of our King
Let's pause to reflect on God's wondrous gift
As softly the carollers sing.

In the rush of the busy days ahead
Come pause at the manger and bow
Let's examine our lives, our thoughts, our souls
And ask the Saviour to show us how—

How we, in this Blessed Christmas hour
And during the whole year through
Can give a gift of meaningful worth
To worship the Christ Child true.

He can't use the gifts we buy
Or the cooking or baking we do
It's not the tree with its lights so bright
But it's you, a part of you.

Let's enter this season with joy and hope
And bring our gifts so rare:
A helping hand, a few kind words,
A willing heart, a silent prayer.

As we give our gifts this Christmas
Like the worshippers of long ago,
May we find the peace Christ promised
When he proved how he loves us so.

Double Blessing
by
Ruth Smith Meyer

The morning of Christmas Eve day, the winter wind whipped the falling snow into huge drifts that reached almost to the top of the railing on the Graves' porch. The furnace valiantly tried to defend the dwelling against sub-zero temperatures. The wind rattled the back door, and a blast of cold air accompanied David Graves as he stepped inside and shut the door with a bang.

"Brr-rr! It's cold enough out there to freeze anything that holds still for a few minutes. It's still snowing too." He brushed the snow from his eyebrows and began to peel off his mitts and parka.

Linda paused her gift wrapping to look up at her husband. "You can hardly see the barn from the south window."

"I'm wondering if I'll have to stretch a rope from house to barn to make sure I don't get lost."

Linda smiled and fussed with a ribbon on top of a large square box. "The pastor called to say that the Christmas Eve service is cancelled. Even if the storm lets up, the roads won't be passable."

Fourteen year-old Janine dropped the package she was carrying onto the table with a thud. "Mom, Dad, if it's storming that much and the roads are closed, how are we going to deliver our Christmas surprise to the Andrews?"

"We have to!" Jaycee and Jacob chimed in unison.

Linda smiled. "Let's pray that the storm will let up in time."

Each year for eight years, the Graves had chosen

a family in need to secretly bless with surprise gifts at Christmas. It pleased Linda that giving the Christmas surprise seemed to equal or even surpass the children's excitement of receiving their own gifts.

This year they had chosen the Andrews family to bless. Rick Andrews had died in a tragic car accident just over a year ago, leaving Karen alone with two sons and a daughter, all under the age of five. Karen worked part time and bravely tried to carry on, but with baby-sitting costs it was hard to make ends meet.

The Graves had a wonderful time choosing clothes and a toy for each of the children. Linda kept her sewing machine busy, making a lovely blouse to go with the sweater they had bought for Karen, as well as extra T-shirts for the children. Janine had pieced together a small comforter made of purple and yellow flannelette for little Janelle Andrews, knotting it with soft purple and light green yarn. The nine-year old twins had helped stuff the sock monkeys for the Andrews boys, and they all had helped bake the Christmas cookies. A box of vegetables and canned goods completed the bundle they planned to deliver tonight.

Linda smiled at her children. "Let's finish wrapping the presents and get everything ready. We'll pack everything into two large garbage bags so it's easier to carry."

Throughout the day, the wind continued to howl. As the family ate supper, they discussed how they could get the Christmas surprise to the Andrews' home given the weather conditions.

"If we just could have Santa's sleigh and the reindeer for a half hour," Jaycee sighed, "we could deliver the gifts even though the roads are closed."

Jacob's eyes twinkled. "Dad, if you had bought that snowmobile I saw advertised, we could have used that!" He added, "Maybe we should get one before next Christmas just in case!"

"Nice try!" David tousled his son's hair. "I think our best solution, assuming the wind lets up, is to take the tractor with attached snow blower. If any drifts are too big I can blow my way through. If worst comes to worst, we'll have to take the gifts Christmas night."

An hour later, it became noticeably quieter outside. Linda went to the window, drawing back the curtains. "Come, look!"

"Hey! The wind has gone down!" Jacob and Jaycee cried in unison.

"The moon is almost breaking through the clouds," added Janine.

"Guess you'd better get dressed in the warmest clothes you can find." Linda put her arm around David's waist. "You'll be a real wise man bearing gifts to Jesus."

"But the gifts aren't for Jesus." Jaycee's wide eyes reflected her confusion.

"But Jesus said that if we give to someone in need, it's like giving to Him," Janine solemnly reminded her little sister. "So, in a way, we are giving gifts to Jesus."

Linda smiled as her heart swelled with thankfulness and pride. *Sometimes they absorb more than we think they do.*

David was busy putting on extra socks. "I'll have to stop a little distance from the Andrews' house or they'll hear the tractor. But I won't be able to ring their doorbell and get away fast enough. Any ideas?"

"I've already thought about that." Linda handed a heavy sweater to her husband. "Melody Kaiser works with Karen. When you're safely back on the tractor, give me a call and I'll phone Melody. I'll ask her if she could contact Karen and tell her to look outside her back door."

Jacob tugged on Linda's hand. "I know it's Christmas Eve, but can we wait to go to bed until Daddy gets home?"

Linda gave him a hug. "Sure. I'll read a few Christmas stories while he's gone."

* * *

Karen Andrews stood at the kitchen sink staring out the window. Choking back the sob that tore at her throat, she squeezed her eyes shut in an attempt to stem the tears that had been threatening to come all afternoon.

You've got to wait until the children are all asleep, she told herself. *It's hard enough for them as it is.*

Last year, the first one without Rick, they had spent Christmas with her parents. This year, work and her old car wouldn't allow that, so her parents had said they'd drive the 250 kilometres to spend the day with her and the children.

The snowstorm had ruined those plans. She and the children would be alone—all alone. She had managed a few dollar store items for the children's stockings, but her parents' bigger gifts would have to wait. How would she explain Santa's stinginess to the children? Another problem was that her parents had planned to bring most of the meal.

Because she could barely keep from crying, she had put the children to bed early. It wasn't hard to get three-year old Trevor and two-year old Janelle to settle down, but Josh had complained. Her suspicion that he was still awake was confirmed when he softly called from his bedroom. "Mom! Come here!"

With a heavy heart, Karen entered his room and sat on his bed. "What's the matter, my little man?"

"Mom, what are we going to do for Christmas tomorrow if Granny and Gramps can't come? Will we still get gifts? What are we going to have for dinner? You said they were going to bring the stuff to go with our chicken…. I wish Daddy was here."

"Josh, darling, I know. I do too. But don't you worry about tomorrow. Remember Jesus is our best gift. It's His birthday and He'll be with us. The gifts may not be big, but there will be something for each of you."

She leaned over to give him a big hug and kissed the top of his head. "Now you need to get to sleep. Okay?"

"Okay, Mom, I'll try."

Karen tucked the blanket around his chin and moved towards the door. "Remember, I love you."

Back in the kitchen, Karen sank onto a chair and leaned her head on her hands.

Dear God, You said You would be with the widows and the fatherless. Where are You tonight?

The tears that had been threatening all day began to flow. *I feel so alone tonight—cut off from everything and everyone that could bring even a semblance of comfort.*

She reached for a tissue and blew her nose. *Lord, You said You'd never leave us or forsake us, but I miss Rick so much and now my parents aren't able to come. I can't even seem to feel Your presence.*

God, are You even listening? Do You care? What about my children? Don't they deserve your attention, even if I don't?

Lord if You do care, can You just send me a little sign? It doesn't need to be a host of angels in the sky—not even a bright star. But please, can You show that You are Emmanuel (God with us) to me?

As she wiped her eyes again, the phone rang. *Oh dear, I hope I won't sound as if I've been crying.*

Answering quickly so that the ringing wouldn't wake the children, she swallowed hard and with great effort to sound cheerful, answered, "Hello?"

"Hi Karen! This is Mel."

"Hi Mel! How are you?"

"I'm fine Karen. I'm your official messenger tonight."

"What do you mean?"

"I just got a call —don't ask me who it was from. I didn't recognize the voice and the lady wouldn't tell me, but she asked me to call you and tell you to look outside your back door."

"What for?"

"I don't know, that's all she would say. Go take a look and tell me what you see. I'll stay on the line until you get back."

"Okay—just a minute."

Karen set the phone down, unlocked the door, and cautiously opened it. There on the porch was a large box of groceries and two big garbage bags. She dragged the bags inside and then lifted the box over the step and slid it into the kitchen too. After shutting the door she picked up the telephone again.

"Melody, you won't believe this, but there's a whole box of groceries and two bags full of packages by the feel of it."

"Oh Karen, isn't that great? I know it's been tough for you."

"But Melody, you don't know the whole story! I just finished praying that God would send me a sign that He hasn't forgotten me." She giggled with embarrassment. "Isn't that silly? In my heart I know He hasn't forgotten me, but I was missing Rick so much, and with my parents not able to come, I was feeling rather lonely and stranded tonight."

"Well, Karen, I'm glad I could play a small part in this, even if I don't know who helped God answer your prayer. I'll let you go and discover what was gifted to you. Give me a call tomorrow sometime. Okay?"

"Will do, Mel. Thanks for being the messenger. I'll talk to you tomorrow."

Excited as a child, Karen opened the bags to find gift-wrapped boxes for each family member. She put the presents around their little garage-sale Christmas tree. She and the children would open the gifts together in the morning. The kids would be so excited.

Karen put the groceries away. It was late and she needed to sleep.

It truly will be Christmas after all, she whispered as

she headed to bed. *But the best gift of all, Heavenly Father, is the way You answered my prayer just at the right time.*

She smiled. *I guess You started on the answer long before I knew I would need it. You have brought me joy and peace and so much more gladness then I expected to feel tonight. Thank You! Thank You!*

Snippets of a verse from "It Came upon a Midnight Clear" floated through her mind: "And ye, beneath life's crushing load/Whose forms are bending low…/Look now! For glad and golden hours/Come swiftly on the wing/O rest beside the weary road/And hear the angels sing!"

Truly, thought Karen sleepily, *I think the angels are singing in my heart.*

The Christmas Tree
by
Tina Markeli

The small island in southeast Asia felt barren. The seemingly lush native jungle hid the harsh truth of the impoverished soil below. Where the jungle had been cleared, the reddish-brown soil grew nothing but tall, harsh grasses. Some properties waiting to be developed sat devoid of any hint of green—for years.

The island's economy boomed, driven, on one hand, by the greed of factory owners and their investors, and on the other, by the desperation of the workers striving to make a living while still sending money home to their families. Like the native jungle, the island's apparent prosperity hid the grinding poverty of the majority.

The indigenous population maintained their traditional fishing lifestyle around the island's rim, but in the central part of the island large chunks of the forest were being cleared away. Newly built factories attracted foreign investment and an abundance of low-cost labour from the many over-populated parts of the country. Housing developments were springing up like popcorn but were usually too expensive for the average factory worker to enjoy.

As many as ten young adults shared a tiny two-bedroom house, with only one bathroom, rolling up their mattresses when they left for their shift so house mates coming home would have room to sleep.

My husband and I had come to this island to help local Christians share their faith and start new churches.

We had seen plenty of poverty in developing countries

over the years, but the barrenness of this island threatened to deaden our souls.

We had found a house to rent in a sub-division just beginning to settle on one of those cleared-of-the-forest areas. None of the original trees had survived the onslaught of the earth movers that had levelled the hillside to make room for houses. A few newly planted trees were bravely trying to take root in the impoverished soil along the main streets, but postage stamp front yards only had room for the family motorcycle and a rack for drying laundry. Plants, if any, were restricted to flower pots on the steps leading to the house. The thousands of factory workers, temporary residents on this island, seldom bothered to plant flowers.

The majority of the population were not Christian; most were tolerant, some were hostile.

Like the trees trying to take root, I led a small neighbourhood Bible study for women who found themselves in this bleak environment and wanted nourishment for their parched souls. One lady, better off than most, offered her house as a meeting place. It was big enough to seat the entire group comfortably on chairs. In a smaller house, we would have sat on mats on the floor. She also provided a welcome snack. We relished these small luxuries.

As the calendar pages announced the coming of Christmas, we eagerly looked for a change from the everyday routine and drab surroundings. Budgets were limited, but the group wanted to celebrate together in some way. A familiar group would help to ease the pain of separation from family and the Christmas traditions these Christian ladies knew.

"I would like you all to come to my house for the next meeting, the one just before Christmas." Mrs. Lilly, a new member and a new believer from a Hindu background, surprised us with her earnest invitation.

We squirmed just a little. In a culture where ancestry and ethnic groups were clearly defined, her fine, long nose, and darker skin, marked her as one not native to the country. Long ago her ancestors had been enticed to come and work as lowly harvesters to collect the sap of the rubber trees, which still grew in vast plantations. She had been born in this country but her race, and therefore she, herself, were outsiders, often despised. Her husband had left her.

We thought she could not afford to serve the meal that was expected for such a celebration. Would she have space for all of us? Would we embarrass her?

But none of this seemed to bother Mrs. Lilly. She had met Jesus and she wanted us to celebrate with her. This was her first Christmas! No cost was too great. Seeing her enthusiasm, the group felt it would be rude to refuse her.

The date was set. We agreed to meet at our usual place and walk together to Mrs. Lilly's home. That would avoid embarrassment if someone came too early or late, or didn't know the way. Doing things together made everyone more comfortable, less threatened by something different.

Our group chatted amiably on the short walk. Before entering the house, we slipped off our shoes, depositing a heap of assorted footwear just outside the door. I immediately spotted the small artificial Christmas tree that dominated the room. Bright decorations of all shapes and colours covered every branch. This tree would never win a best-colour-coordinated award. By western standards, it was a candidate for "worst tree of the year," a gaudy riot of colour, the complete opposite of the grey cement block houses and brown landscape beyond the window.

Over-decorated but so typical of this lady's ethnic group. The words sprang into my mind, unbidden. I knew I shouldn't criticize. Still, why had she spent money on meaningless decorations? She could have used the money to feed her children. Someone really should tell her that Christmas is about Christ, not about the tree or its trimmings. My thoughts tumbled themselves into a tight knot. Mentally, I put a clamp on my lips, an extra-firm clamp.

It would be best to wait, listen, and ask questions before I stated my opinion, an opinion formed by my German-Canadian heritage.

We seated ourselves around the room, taking up every chair. They had obviously been carefully counted before our arrival. We sang the beloved Christmas carols with enthusiasm, hoping that just a little of their message would find its way into the world beyond the walls. Together we listened to God's Word, letting it water our thirsty souls. We prayed that our hearts would be fertile soil for the truths of Christmas, that we would live as faithful Christ-followers. In the midst of long work hours, low wages and high prices, never enough money, and the separation from our families that numbed our souls, how could we share the message of Christ's coming with those who didn't know Him? With those who were hostile to our faith?

"I'm going to get some more decorations for my tree as soon as I get some more money," our hostess proclaimed eagerly.

My heart sank. The tree was already groaning under the weight of decorations. Where could she possibly find space to hang even one more bauble? She had so many other needs—school uniforms, books, and fees, not to mention food for her children. Maybe I should take her aside after the meeting and say something; but what could I possibly say that would not deeply offend her?

Fortunately, our hostess was unaware of the thoughts fighting for control in my mind. Her serious expression added the weight of firm conviction to each word. "In this community, only Christians put up Christmas trees. I want everyone in the neighbourhood to know that I have become a follower of Jesus. I will make my tree as full of decorations as I possibly can so that people will see how much I love Jesus. It is my love gift to Him." Her eyes shone bright.

Like a giant earth mover clearing the jungle, God

bulldozed through my swirling, tangled knot of thoughts. This new believer had seen something that I had missed completely. She was right. Christmas decorations in our housing complex had real significance. I had never noticed. I had simply transferred my own decorating ideas from Canada to a new location. The manger scene with Mary, Joseph, and the baby Jesus told the Christmas story, of course. But other decorations? Well, those were just traditions, comforting reminders of Christmas in Canada. I had allowed the jungle of my traditions to hide the needs and opportunities in my neighbourhood from my eyes.

My new point of view transformed my morning walks around the complex. I took notice of the houses with Christmas decorations—bold statements of joy and faith in our sometimes hostile, always-drab environment. Knowing that there were other believers nearby filled my heart with great joy. I prayed that their faith would be demonstrated in daily actions, not merely in their decorations. Where I saw no signs of Christmas, I prayed that the residents would come to know the Saviour.

In the multi-cultural Canadian neighbourhood where I now live, I need to remember that Christmas decorations, or their absence, is a signal to pray just as in southeast Asia. A nativity scene in our front window, one of only two in our townhouse complex, tells our neighbours the meaning of Christmas and calls me to pray for them.

My sister's sacrifice and eager declaration, years ago, were God's earth movers to clear my mind for something new. Christmas trees are no longer mere decorations. They are a summons to prayer.

Christmas Firsts

by

Pat Gerbrandt

The doll was only $3.98! Was it unusual for a first-grader to look for the lowest priced doll in the Eaton's Christmas catalogue? Perhaps. Even the sudden longing for a doll was a surprise. I usually preferred to play with trucks and cars, but when I saw the baby dolls in the catalogue, I began to long for a new doll. There were many firsts that year for me, as well as for my parents.

We had moved into town from a farm, so my mom could be closer to her mother and father. My grandparents' move from their farm into Winkler just a few years earlier, in the late 1940s, had not been easy for my grandmother, and Mom was the only one close enough to offer help. Grandpa had his books and newspapers, and loved to visit. Grandma missed the outdoor farm work.

It wasn't the first time we lived in a cheap rental house, but for the first time I became aware of differences between our neighbours' houses and ours. The well-kept one-storey houses, pristine in fresh paint, one on each side of us, made our taller, unpainted, gray two-storey house conspicuous. It didn't particularly bother me then, but I knew it was different.

Another first was attending a large public school. I had only two months in the small stone building in the country where two grades were combined in one classroom before we left the farm.

In town I walked to school. There I could play with friends after school because we lived close enough to walk to each other's homes. Another first, I could walk to my

74

grandparents' house with Mom. As a six year old, I enjoyed these firsts.

Everything seemed new and exciting to my carefree spirit. It was different for my parents. Responsibility must have weighed heavily on them. Daddy worked on road and bridge construction crews in the summer time, but winter was slow. I see now that his crabbiness, his occasional out-bursts of anger, and his morose moping were signs of slight depression. Daddy was a perfectionist. Although he had many creative abilities and worked hard, there were times the high standards he held for himself as well as for others led to disagreements and frustration. He wanted so badly to provide for us and often felt he was a failure.

I was excited to learn that I could take home the Christmas tree from my first grade classroom when school let out for the holidays. Daddy didn't seem too pleased. I had no idea this showed we were poor. Mom said Grandpa and Grandma had decided not to decorate a tree that year, so she brought home their old multicolored lights and the shimmery angel tree topper that I thought was the most beautiful decoration. Mom and I strung some popped corn to add to the wrinkled tinsel. It was our first tree, and I thought it was perfect!

Meanwhile, Mom bravely kept on doing what she could. She visited her parents, helping them with meal preparation, laundry, mending, and, sometimes, just by being there. At home, she baked bread and prepared our meals. Sometimes, my supper was bread crumbled into a bowl of milk. It was a special treat for me, but I don't remember Mom and Dad eating that. Did they wait until I was in bed to ease their hunger with bread and coffee? Years later, Mom admitted she didn't give me that simple supper only because I liked it so much. There just wasn't always enough money for groceries. Mom also sewed all her own clothes and mine, and used scraps of those fabrics to make clothes for my red-haired doll.

Now I wonder whether she was trying to help me

appreciate the doll I already had, deflect my pleas for the baby doll, or both!

Mom did warn me not to get my hopes up. I think she even explained that we did not have a lot of money. That's when I realized even a $3.98 doll might be too expensive. I put the catalogue away and tried not to think about the baby doll.

One evening, Mom asked me to get some potatoes from the cellar. I didn't like being in that damp, dark space, so I grabbed the potatoes and hurried back up the ladder. Daddy seemed upset.

"What did you see downstairs?"

See? I didn't take time to look, except to make sure that there were no salamanders. They sometimes crept out of the earthen walls.

Christmas Eve came, and we went to church for the Sunday School Christmas program.

When we got home, my parents told me to go into the front room. We didn't usually use that room, and the door was kept closed in an attempt to keep precious heat from seeping away from the rest of the house. There, in the corner, under the tree, was a cloth-covered lump. Daddy and Mom urged me to lift the cover. My doll! It was the baby doll I'd yearned for. The cloth cover was a square of pink flannel Mom had hemmed and trimmed by hand with darker pink blanket-stitch. Daddy admitted he'd asked what I saw in the cellar because he'd been working down there, secretly building a bed for my doll. He'd bought a bit of wooden dowelling and a few thin pieces of wood to combine with other supplies he had found in the shed, and lovingly crafted a bed the perfect size for my new baby doll.

The Christmas I received my baby doll and the doll bed was the first time I began to understand sacrificial love. My parents never told me their gift was a lesson in God's redemptive love, but the doll and the bed have reminded me ever since, and I'm grateful for all these gifts.

A Night to Remember
by

Janet Seever

"It doesn't seem like Christmas season," I remarked to my husband, Dennis. "I guess if we want a Christmas tree this year, we'll have to use a banana tree." Instead of the gently falling snow and frosted windows of my Minnesota childhood, tropical downpours pelted our metal roof nightly with a deafening roar. Daytime temperatures soared into the low 30s and the humidity was high.

We had been in Papua New Guinea as missionaries for six months and were adjusting to being away from friends and family for the first time. However, the prospect of holidays without loved ones brought a new wave of homesickness. I couldn't even play my Christmas music tapes because our broken tape recorder was being repaired.

Then an invitation to a children's Christmas program arrived. A month earlier, the international school in town had contacted me when they urgently needed a substitute teacher for a couple of days. As a result, we were invited to the elementary school's Christmas program, and I eagerly accepted. I wanted to see the children I had taught, but more than that, I was eager for something that reflected Christmas, since they would be singing Christmas carols as part of the program.

We normally rode our motorcycle into town during the day, but tonight we borrowed a van from friends. Jeannette, who worked with another mission down the road, wanted to ride with us.

The evening was a lovely diversion from the many

nights we spent at home. We enjoyed the singing, and visiting with other expatriate families afterwards was a high point of our week.

When we began our eight-kilometre journey home several hours later, the nightly rain had already started. The swish of the windshield wipers kept a steady pace as the van creaked and rattled along. Dennis carefully dodged the potholes.

We had gone about five kilometres when suddenly our pleasant conversation came to an abrupt halt. As we rounded a bend, lanterns flashed in the darkness, and about twenty shouting and waving Papua New Guinea villagers blocked the road ahead of us.

My muscles tensed as I peered through the rain-spattered windshield. "What do they want?" I asked. These were not people we wanted to encounter in the dark. We had been told that during World War II—more than thirty years earlier—inhabitants of this village aided Japanese soldiers, and they were later severely punished by the Australian government ruling Papua New Guinea at that time. For that reason, these villagers hated all white people.

The spokesman for the group told us in broken English that a tree had struck the bridge up ahead. All three of us in the van collectively breathed a sigh of relief—the villagers were only trying to warn us. The human road-block moved aside, and let us pass.

Dennis inched the van slowly forward. How much damage had been done? Could we still get across? Jeannette lived on the other side of the creek and we still had a couple of kilometres to go beyond that before we reached home.

Our headlights soon revealed the problem. The shallow stream we crossed three hours earlier had become a raging torrent, fed by heavy rain in the mountains. Many of the large trees growing along the creek had shallow root systems and were easily uprooted when the water rose.

One of these uprooted trees had rammed the bridge and lay partly over the top of it. The road now ended abruptly with a three-metre drop where swirling brown water had eroded a yawning hole. A four-metre gap separated the road from the bridge, rendering it completely useless.

We surveyed the situation with dismay, not wanting to spend the night there. But there was no way to get across.

"I have an idea," said Jeanette. "We could leave the van here and walk across the new bridge." She got her flashlight out from under the seat of the van. "Our mission is only about 400 metres farther."

The new two-lane bridge, eight metres high, was well above the water level. It ran parallel to the old one and had been under construction for the past seven months. All it needed was the railings.

After Dennis backed up the van and parked it on the muddy shoulder of the road, we all got out. By now the villagers were beginning to construct a barricade with fifty-five gallon drums to prevent anyone from accidentally driving into the swirling water.

The road leading to the new bridge was not yet gravelled, so clods of clay clung to our shoes. The rain had lessened to a gentle mist. Using Jeanette's flashlight to guide us, we slowly started to cross. The angry water roared below us as brush and boulders crashed into the steel bridge pilings.

"Lord, keep us safe," I prayed. "Please help us get home."

The bridge seemed to stretch on endlessly. We could see its outline through the mist as the beam of light bounced off the wet concrete in front of us. Then Jeannette's flashlight started to flicker.

Suddenly we froze in our tracks. Five metres in front of us, there was no more bridge or road—just swirling water eight metres below! The raging water had changed its course and washed out about fifteen metres of landfill and road leading up to the bridge.

With knees shaking and a nearly dead flashlight, we carefully retraced our steps to the parked van.

Then Jeannette had another idea. "A new family just moved into our mission's administrative headquarters near town," she said. "We might be able to spend the night there."

"Good idea," said Dennis. "But first I think we should let the police know the bridge is out." He eased the van out of the mud and headed back to town.

We had gone a couple of kilometres and were nearing town when we discovered two huge trees—the kind with shallow root systems—had fallen across the road we had just travelled thirty minutes earlier.

I gasped. "If we had turned back any sooner we might have been under those trees!"

"The Lord was really watching over us," said Jeannette, echoing the sentiment we all felt.

We spent the night in the mission house as Jeannette had suggested, and the next afternoon the water subsided enough for us to wade across the knee-deep muddy stream.

We learned that bamboo houses had been swept away in several villages, leaving 400 homeless, and one elderly woman had drowned. The water had enough force to move boulders two metres in diameter.

Later I shared the terrifying experience with a friend, but he seemed unimpressed. "A lot of people have narrow escapes every day. Nothing happened to you. It was just an inconvenience not to get home."

Nothing happened? Just an inconvenience? I was indignant. But then I saw what he meant. We had been warned in time and hadn't driven off the bank, we weren't in any real danger of falling off the bridge, and half a forest could have fallen across the road in the time we were gone.

There was no miraculous rescue.

So nothing happened that terrifying night—or did it? I am the kind of person who imagines the worst in every situation and could see myself being swept away by raging water or trapped under a fallen tree. What did happen is that I got to know the Lord and His abiding presence in a new way that night. It was as if He tapped me on the shoulder and whispered, "I was right there with you all the time, just as I promised."

Thank you, Lord, for being our Emmanuel—God with us—in the difficult times of life.

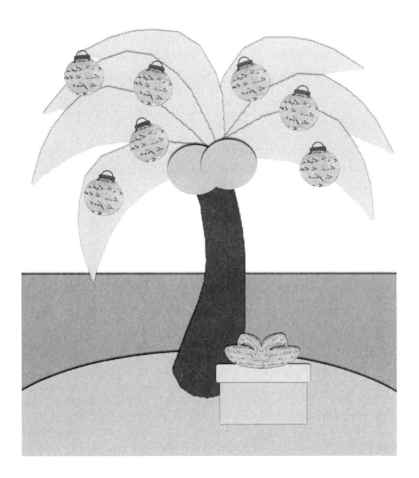

A Belated Christmas Present
by
Elaine Ingalls Hogg

Christmas Season, December 30, 2015

Dearest Friends and Family,

As I write this, I am remembering some of the Christmas celebrations in the past, which included many of you. So many happy occasions, all of which made me thankful even when this year's memories haven't been all joyous.

This December has presented several challenges, one of which was my dad's admittance to hospital after a fall in his home earlier in the month. He still isn't doing well. My youngest brother and his wife have visited often, and another brother and his wife have arrived home from Victoria to see him and support our mom.

Sometimes in our post-visit discussions, we've wondered whether Dad has given up. I'm not sure, but I do know he is weak—weak to the point where he can't move on his own, finds it hard to eat, and doesn't have the strength or energy to open the big red bag containing his Christmas presents.

While visiting the hospital today, I was shaken when I entered his room. It was empty. The bed was stripped and I could see none of his personal belongings. I scurried to the nurses' station, feeling bewildered. Where was he?

"He's in the TV room," the receptionist said.

I followed her directions and found my mom bending over my dad's still form. He was lying down, sleeping on the sofa. One glance confirmed how much his health has failed this year, even more so since he was admitted to institutional care.

Sparkling tinsel, vivid red poinsettia, and twinkling lights lent an air of Christmas to the room; but Dad slept on, unaware of his surroundings.

I felt a tear pushing for an escape route and I swallowed hard. Mom moved to Dad's side and touched his arm. He struggled to open his eyes. On the first day of his hospital stay, when Mom tried to wake him, he had bellowed, "Leave me alone." This time there was no shout, just a faint whisper. "Who are you?" He looked at us, but gave no indication he recognized anyone.

Mom stepped back and drew in a deep breath. "It's Elaine and Hugh," she said, pointing to us. Then she asked, "And you know who I am, don't you?"

"Oh yes, Elaine and Hugh." He smiled weakly then dropped his head back on the sofa and fell back to sleep without responding to Mom's question.

We pulled up chairs and made a semicircle around his sleeping form.

I thought of playing the piano for him, but the TV in the corner blared and I didn't want to disturb the man who had his wheelchair parked fifteen centimetres in front of it. I slipped out of the room and went back to the desk to ask the receptionist if there was a good time to play a couple of pieces for my dad.

"Oh, just play," she said. "The TV is on to keep the residents company, but they like it better when someone plays the piano."

I went back and ran my fingers over the keys. The piano was rustier than me and badly out of tune. I hesitated. A thought romped through my head. Will my playing bother my dad who has perfect pitch and always minded it when someone sang or played an instrument that was flat or sharp?

I decided to play a Christmas piece and gauge his reaction. Halfway through the carol, I noticed he moved his thin, bony hands together as if clasped in prayer, but his eyes remained closed. On my right, someone in a wheelchair moved closer to the piano. The occupant started to sing the words of "Silent Night." Although it was not on pitch and about a measure behind the music, it was a joyous noise. The cacophony of sound bore the resemblance of a late night bar scene, but the expression on her face spoke of the joy she felt in her heart.

More people joined in. Realizing I had a gathering audience and Dad didn't seem to be minding the tuneless melody, I continued to play. When I exhausted my Christmas repertoire, I played "What a Friend We Have in Jesus." Part way through the song I heard a faint noise. I looked over to where Dad was stretched out on the sofa. His eyes were still closed, but he looked relaxed and peaceful. Slowly, deliberately, he raised his hands towards Heaven and sang in a still clear voice, "Have you trials and temptations; is there trouble anywhere? We should never be discouraged. Take it to the Lord in prayer."

Throughout his life, Dad has faithfully trusted God to provide for his family. When I was seven and he broke his leg, our family had to move to a different town to find less physically demanding work; yet he trusted God to meet his needs. He trusted God to take care of his children during their illnesses and to take care of the bills when in his mid-forties he had to move west because jobs were scarce in the Maritimes and the cupboard was bare. Every morning from the day I was born until his recent illness, my dad has prayed for my brothers and me by name.

Yes, I'll admit some days this year have felt especially dark and heavy; but today's Bible verses challenged me to look for joy in the Valley of Weeping.

"What joy for those whose strength comes from the Lord, who have set their minds on a pilgrimage to Jerusalem. When they walk through the Valley of Weeping, it will become a place of refreshing springs. The autumn rains will clothe it with blessings" *(Psalm 84:5-6, NLT).*

Now, as I look back on my day, I realize I have received a belated Christmas present. In this short, impromptu concert, I experienced a true taste of Christmas joy—the kind of joy one only experiences when we take the time to give to others.

And as I close my greetings to each of you dear ones, I pray that whenever you face uncertain days in the New Year, draw comfort from your faith knowing that God will be your constant companion and guide you through each day—even if the day seems like you are walking through the Valley of Weeping.

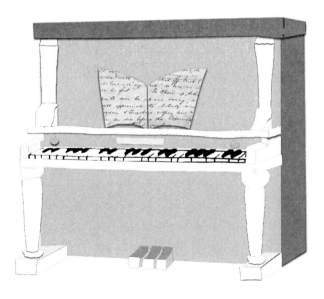

Orange-Coloured Memories
by
Tandy Balson

My earliest Christmas memories are not of coloured lights or gifts under the tree. They are not even of fun and laughter shared at family gatherings. Instead, they are of something I looked forward to with great anticipation. The sweet smell made my mouth water and I could hardly wait to have a bite of the juicy goodness.

It may sound strange, but my fond memories are of a fruit that came in little wooden boxes. Mandarin oranges seemed like an exotic treat because they were available for so short a time.

I grew up in a family of five children. My sister, Barb, fourteen years older, was living on her own when I was very young, so she posed no competition for these treats. Two older brothers, Dave and Rob, were teenagers and could devour a box of oranges in an afternoon, leaving none for my little brother Tim and me.

To ensure everyone got their fair share, my mom would purchase a separate box for Tim and me. I clearly remember her counting the oranges in the box and dividing them evenly between us. Mom warned us, "This is all you will get. It's up to you when you eat them, but you need to know, if you eat them all today, there won't be any more."

I took this to heart and hid the bag of oranges in my room, determined to enjoy them for as long as possible. Tim tried to make his last, but they were so tasty, he'd soon finish his share. Before long, he'd be at my bedroom door begging for just one more.

There was no way I was going to part with any of mine. It wasn't fair to expect me to look favourably on him just because he was only five and I was eight. Tim would ask Mom to make me share. She'd patiently explain that he knew the rules and I could do whatever I wanted with my oranges.

I remember seeing an extra box of oranges that we weren't allowed to touch. There was no explanation and one day the whole box was missing. Later, one of my older brothers shed some light on this mystery. He said Mom had told him he couldn't open this box because Dad was taking it to the renters.

Our dad rented a small house to a single mom with young children. Mandarin oranges were expensive and he knew they couldn't afford them. Dad wanted them to enjoy this treat as much as we did, so he was going to deliver the box to them. In my brother Rob's words, "Our greedy little pleading faces had no impact on him whatsoever."

Dad ensured we had all we needed and then quietly shared the abundance with others less fortunate. If Mom hadn't told us, we never would have known of his generosity.

My quiet, unassuming dad unknowingly taught me to give without seeking attention. To some, giving a box of oranges may not seem like a big deal. To that family, it showed someone cared.

Christmas is a time when people openly show compassion and generosity. I had the opportunity to witness a modest example of this, and is the reason that some of my fondest Christmas memories revolve around mandarin oranges.

And yes, I did eventually give in and share with my little brother. Not because I had to, but because I learned how good it feels to freely share.

87

Traditions at the End of the World

by

Kim Louise Clarke

The car radio was playing "O Christmas Tree." When it came to the line about the leaves being inviting, my son became critical.

"Evergreens have needles. Not leaves."

He was not in a good mood, but then he was a teenager and I was driving him to the dentist. After his appointment, we were to meet up with my husband and daughter and together go out on our yearly expedition to find a Christmas tree—a lovely evergreen with beautiful branches and needles.

Sitting in the waiting room mindlessly skimming magazines, I was not caught up with cavities, flossing, or x-rays. My concern centred on Christmas trees, knowing that a number of tree lots in the city were already sold out. It was December 21, 2012. I don't know how the time had gotten away on us. We had never been this late buying a tree before.

Today was the winter solstice, the shortest day of the year, which added a psychological gloominess, reminding me that we had less daylight to accomplish anything at all. My son informed me that according to the Mayan calendar, today's ominous date of 12-21-12 signified the end of the world. So, while time was short in many ways, apparently to some people it was very short indeed. He also mentioned that as far as tree shopping with the family was concerned, he had little time to spare because he and his friends had plans to go to an "end-of-the-world" party.

The receptionist stood up and began taking down the festive stockings that hung from the desk. She explained that my son's appointment was the second last one scheduled that day. In fact it was the second last one for the year. The office would be closing in just over an hour, until the first week of January.

"I don't want to return to it looking like Christmas!" she said.

She took down the plastic 3-D Santa from the wall and collected the greeting cards from the counter top. She came towards the small white glimmering tree that stood on the table beside me. How strange to see a Christmas tree unplugged, wrapped up, and plopped into a box, when I had yet to get a tree, let alone decorate it. It made me wonder why I had become so anxious about getting something that so soon would be undecorated and tossed outside to be recycled.

Within minutes the Christmas look had disappeared and soon after my son and I walked out of the sterile dental office with its beige walls. We met my husband and daughter at the Real Canadian Superstore. The huge entrance, once a forest of tightly wrapped evergreens, had become a barren metal framework where the cold wind trapped spruce remnants, pine needles, and shreds of plastic wrapping in the corners and whipped them up with the snow. Back in the van, I noted my husband's expression as he listened on his cell phone and I knew that other superstores must also be sold out.

In past years, we had bought Christmas trees from my husband's old Boy Scout troop at their lot behind St. Cyprian's Church. Ever hopeful, we drove there and pulled into the ominously empty parking lot. Everything was locked up tight. All the trees had been sold. The place was abandoned.

On this winter solstice afternoon, the sun had reached its peak long before and was about to disappear altogether. We thought about trying Costco. Should we go there? They have everything. My husband and I did not hold high hopes. I knew my daughter did not want to give up, living up to one of her middle names, "Hope." But our son had to get to his end-of-the-world party and could no longer join us on our quest for a Christmas tree.

This wasn't the most important family tradition we held, but somehow it was always something we managed to do together as a family—until now. I knew I was blessed with a family that enjoyed doing certain things together at Christmas time. We attended the Christmas Eve service at church, then on Christmas morning our kids woke up to filled stockings, no matter how old they got, and later that day we enjoyed a turkey dinner. On Boxing Day our house filled with family and friends.

So, while buying a tree had always been a small, rather unorganized family tradition, I felt it was being broken. Of course, I realized that it wasn't the end of the world. My children were simply growing up and I needed to let that happen.

We dropped off our son, and the rest of us headed over to Costco. On arrival we found that my husband had left his wallet at home, and although I had my wallet, I didn't have my Costco card. We couldn't see any trees outside for sale anyway.

The temperature dropped as the evening hours set in. Across the way stood a Canadian Tire store with no visible tree lot. We drove there. By this time, I think we had all reached the conclusion that buying a real tree had become impossible. Another family tradition was about to end and I began to feel a real sense of loss. It was a little bit like the end of the world. We have always had a real Christmas tree. It was all I had ever known growing up, and all my children had ever known. Now we were about to look at artificial trees.

The first thing one usually sees upon entering Canadian Tire at this time of year is a brilliant colourful forest. Today, in the middle of that forest, a sign indicated that all artificial trees had been reduced in price. I had to face it—it was a sign. If I read between the lines on the sale sign, it would say to be grateful and not so stuck in your ways, because an artificial tree is not the end of the world.

One tree especially caught our attention. A just-under two-metre floor model stood very pretty with sparkling warm white lights and a price tag reading an incredible $29.99. An employee searched for its box, but it had vanished. Once it was separated into its three parts, my husband, daughter, and I each carried a portion out to our van.

While driving home I thought about the downside of our decision. We'd miss the lovely scent of spruce or pine filling the house. Nothing could replace that, but pine-scented candles might help capture a sense of the outdoors. Then I remembered that the year before we'd bought an expensive new tree stand that could hold gallons of water. So much for that. However, having an artificial tree meant that I wouldn't need to water it, and let's face it, I was the one who always took care of that job. I was the one who worried that if the tree didn't get enough water, it would dry out, catch fire, and burn our house down. But now with an artificial tree, I was free.

Once home, we set up our perfectly symmetrical tree, and I marvelled at how tree sap didn't get on my hands and needles didn't spread across the floor. When we plugged in the tree, we found that the bottom string of lights, which lit up so beautifully in the store, no longer worked. What happened? No matter. We had no time to take it back. The simple answer was to remove the bottom string, but after ten minutes of exhausting effort, I had only managed to pry two little lights off a branch. I gave up and left the removal of the dead string of lights as a project for next year. Meanwhile we added other lights and all our decorations.

The shortest day of the year drifted into the late evening hours. It had indeed been a very long day. The next day, December 22, the sun rose and streamed in on a beautifully adorned Christmas tree in our front room. The world had not ended.

It's been five years since that Christmas and we have the same artificial tree, which I've come to love. Every year in early December, I make three easy trips down to our basement storage room and then set up our tree.

We still celebrate through many of our same family traditions. But every year we experience a few changes because our family changes and grows. We have learned to rejoice each year as various events occur. We celebrate and rejoice just as God told the Israelites to do. *"Rejoice in all the good things the Lord your God has given to you and your household" (Deuteronomy 26:11b).*

I am learning to hold traditions loosely and allow room for change. It's always a challenge to let change in, but when I make room for it, it frees me up and allows me to grow in different directions through new experiences. Change may be scary at times, but it is never the end of the world.

I am reminded that it is best to hold tightly onto Christ who *"is the same yesterday and today and forever" (Hebrews 13:8).* It is always Jesus Christ who we can count on through all the changes that happen to us and around us. He is the constant in Christmas. He is always there, year after year, the One we celebrate at Christmas time, the One upholding us as we honour Him through the Christmas season.

Have I Told You Lately That I Love You?

by

M. Eleanor Maisey

As told by Edna Ferguson

It was at our 1976 family reunion when my brother, Barry, came over to me and plunked a dusty old cardboard box on my lap. "Sis, I think you will like this."

Puzzled, I gingerly lifted the lid and peeked inside. I threw up my hands and cried, "Well, here's my Suzie."

In my excitement, the box started to slip off my knee but I caught it before it fell. Then I took a closer look at my old Eaton Beauty doll. Her eyes were closed, and she looked like she was asleep lying there. Pearly white teeth peeked through her smile and the chubby cheeks still had a few dark curls around them. I reached in to pick her up but she fell apart. The sturdy elastic that had held her limbs together had disintegrated over time.

Years earlier, when I had left home for Bible College, my mother had tucked my doll into that cardboard box and pushed it between the rafters in the attic of our old farmhouse. Later, insulation was blown into the attic and it was sealed shut. That insulation was removed when my brother remodelled the old home and he found the box. He checked its contents and thought of me.

I took my doll home and began putting her back together again. I remembered her well, but since I wanted her to look like she did originally, I contacted our local museum for help. They showed me the number that was pressed on the back of Suzie's neck and then brought out a doll from their collection. Its number matched Suzie's so that confirmed that she was the 1926 Eaton's doll. I was ready to get my doll back to the way she looked when I first got her.

I spent a fair bit of money on a replacement wig, socks, and little black shoes. Those little shoes cost almost as much as my own! I made the tiny pink satin dress so it looked just like the one I remembered. I felt the time and money I'd spent restoring her was a labour of love, since she was to be a Christmas gift for my only daughter, Sharon. I also made a recording of my happy childhood memories for her.

When Suzie finally looked like she had in 1926, I put her on the bed in our spare room where I could admire her and occasionally give her a hug. She was about fifty-three centimetres long, so she actually looked just like a real baby. Sometimes I took her with me for children's church. She was a big hit, especially with the girls.

I grew up on a small farm in southern Saskatchewan during the depression. Money was scarce in our home, but we were happy. Mother made many of the clothes my siblings and I wore. Dad made most of the toys we played with.

Our family's trips to town were planned events, a time when our parents bought only family necessities and then picked up the mail. Sometimes the mail contained an Eaton's catalogue, but our parents sent mail orders strictly for things that were not available in town.

Early each fall, we kids eagerly watched for the Eaton's Christmas catalogue. It was a happy diversion with its colourful pages of children's toys, and we spent hours poring over those pages. Soon they were dog-eared from use.

We never knew when mother mailed the Christmas order. But when a big Eaton's parcel came with the mail, Dad carried it into the house and mother quickly whisked it out of sight. It contained secrets!

I was six years old in 1926 and desperately wanted a doll of my own. Eaton's catalogue featured a different doll every year, but I thought that year's doll was the most beautiful one yet. Somehow, I just knew she was going to be mine that coming Christmas.

I remember going to the kitchen one day where mother was busy preparing supper. I held the catalogue so the page with the Eaton's doll was showing. I patiently waited until I had her attention and then asked if I could please have that doll for Christmas.

Mother's quick glance and noncommittal, "We'll see," didn't discourage me one bit. I was afraid I knew what her answer would be, but I still hoped, prayed, and waited. I was so sure I would get my Eaton Beauty doll.

The doll cost about $1.98, which doesn't seem like much today, but now I realize how difficult it was for our parents to clothe and feed our family during the depression. Grain prices were low and weather was always a worry. So mother supplemented our farm income by raising chickens and selling the eggs for five cents a dozen. She churned butter too, and sold it for ten cents a pound (half kilogram). However, our parents shielded us kids from their financial concerns. We were adults before we knew of their personal sacrifices.

Our kitchen was small, so all our meals were eaten in the dining room. A big, black, pot-bellied stove dominated one corner of the room to heat it. We had no Christmas tree in 1926, since we lived on the bald prairie. However, each year when the Christmas season approached, everyone in the family got into the act. We twisted red and green crepe paper streamers together and then strung them from corner to corner. The streamers met over the centre of the dining room table, where they rested on a big hook that hung from the ceiling. After, Dad hung a huge, red, crepe paper bell from that hook. I remember causing no little excitement that Christmas night when I accidentally set the bell on fire. But that's another story.

On Christmas Eve we kids hung one of our stockings on the back of our chair for Santa to fill. On Christmas morning there would be an orange in the toe of our sock, colourful hard candies piled on top of it, and a piece of mother's shortbread. Santa got a piece of shortbread too.

My younger sister, Violet, and I shared a bed and we went to bed early that Christmas Eve. However, we were much too excited to sleep right away. I just knew that I would get my doll. I even said an extra prayer for her that night, just in case. Violet and I finally drifted off to sleep but I woke early, nudged Violet awake with my cold foot and whispered, "Let's go see what Santa brought us!"

We slid out of bed onto the icy wood floor, not even stopping to put on slippers. We crept along the hallway to the dining room, stopped at the doorway and just stared. Our dining room was bathed in a soft orange glow from the flame in the big stove. Dad had banked it with coal the night before. Our stockings hung from the chair backs, sagging from the treats they held. It was a memorable scene.

Violet and I stood holding hands, shivering from chill and excitement. We could hardly believe our eyes. Tucked in my little rocking chair sat two Eaton Beauty dolls. "We got them," we cried and ran to pick them up. But, we were stopped short from dad's booming voice.

"You girls get back to bed or you won't get any-thing!" We scampered to our room, jumped into bed, and pulled the comforter over our heads. The two of us lay there, giggling, hugging each other, and listening for Mother's call to breakfast.

Christmas morning in our home began like any other day. Dad and my brothers cared for the animals and did the milking while Mother made breakfast. We ate in the dining room, as usual, but the decorations made the meal special. When breakfast was over and the dishes cleared away, Dad read the Christmas story from the Gospel of Luke. Violet and I sat fidgeting, trying hard to concentrate on the story and ignore the gifts nearby, especially our dolls.

Finally, Dad said a prayer of thanksgiving and it was time to open our parcels. There were not a lot of them, but the gifts we received were special, since our parents did their best to give us the things we wanted most.

Suzie was precious to me. I loved her, hugged her and kissed her, played with her, and told her all kinds of secrets. I even slept with her. But not once did she ever tell me she loved me or hug me or kiss me or tell me a secret. After all, she was just a doll! Now I sometimes wonder, how many times I have been just like that doll and not told my family that I loved and appreciated each one of them?

I remember the day I told this story in children's church. One little girl listened intently. When I finished, she jumped up from her seat and rushed back two pews, threw her arms around the lady sitting there and exclaimed, "I love you Gram." Then she walked back to her place and smiled at Suzie and me. She understood that God's greatest gift at Christmas is love.

Canela Nativity Scene
by

Jack D. Popjes

Translating the Bible into an unwritten, unknown language is difficult—really difficult. But there is something that is even more problematic: answering the question, "What do readers and hearers understand?"

After years of studying the language and culture of the Canela people of Brazil and becoming accepted members of Canela society, my wife Jo and I were finally translating the Gospel of Luke. Our training had prepared us to do this, and we had some bright Canela translation helpers.

While we were the Bible experts, they were the language experts—we made a team that worked well together. The translation part was difficult, but doable.

Now came the hardest part—testing each newly translated portion to see if it communicated clearly.

Several tools helped us. We read the passage to someone who had never heard it before and asked him or her to tell what he/she had just heard in his/her own words. We also probed their understanding by asking follow-up questions. If there were problems, the translation had to be revised.

Another, more popular, culturally appropriate checking tool for the drama-loving Canela was to give a group of young people the printout of a parable of Jesus, or some other action narrative, and ask them to act it out. It was hilarious to see them perform the parable of the sower. Some young women, acting as the seed that fell on stony ground, grew up rapidly but then slumped weakly back down to the ground. Other girls, acting as seeds, were picked up by strong young men who carried them off while cawing as ravens.

We were wondering how best to check the Christmas story when we thought of a young Canela artist who had drawn illustrations for a reading exercise book on local birds that Jo had written and published. Drawing

98

a picture was another good checking tool. We gave him a printout of Luke's Christmas story, a black ballpoint pen, and some paper and asked him to read the story, then pick out a scene to illustrate.

A few days later he returned with a drawing of a very typical Canela birth scene—a young mother sitting on her platform bed, holding her baby, with the father watching over them. All very Canela—except for the addition of some farm animals and a donkey by a feeding trough. None of these would appear in a Canela house.

Yes! He got it. Jesus was born in a stable, not in a house.

We kept on translating for many years. Finally, in the last five years of the translation program, the Good News suddenly exploded among the Canelas and dozens of young men and women began to follow Jesus—the Baby who came to live, die, and rise again from the dead to be their Saviour and Chief.

Currently, scores of Canela men, women, and children are reading and following the teaching of God's Word in their own language. They are still solidly Canela, speaking their native language and maintaining their own cultural distinctives. But they now trust in Jesus, the Son of their Great Father in the Sky, and His Powerful Spirit, who protects them from the evil one and his malevolent spirits.

God now shows Himself clearly to the Canelas as they read an accurate translation of His Word in their own language.

99

Christmas-A Time For Thanksgiving?

by

Charleen Raschke

It was the mid-1990s, and the Christmas season was upon us. We loaded up our old GMC van, bundled up our three young children, and began our journey. It was going to be a very long day, travelling through the Rocky Mountains to be with our family on the Prairies of Western Canada.

The kids were troopers. They travelled well, entertaining themselves and each other. They sang along to our cassettes and listened intently to many different stories on tape. Excitement built inside the vehicle the closer we got to Grandma and Grandpa's farm. This yearly tradition never got old.

We always anticipated good food, reconnecting with aunts, uncles, cousins, and grandparents, and the many games we would play. Upon arrival our two older kids piled out of the van, as did our Bassett Hound, Sam. Grandpa's Arabian stallion, Rocky, threw his head in the air as he pranced around his pen and the Blue Heeler, Ricky, did his happy dance as he greeted us. There were exuberant hugs all around.

My husband and I took a little longer helping our youngest son with special needs into the house, as he needed us to carry him. Loads of luggage were brought inside, as we settled into the parts of the house we would claim as our own over the coming days.

A mingling of smells—coffee brewing and fresh

baking—heightened our senses. Grandma was quick to offer something to eat and drink. Her gift of hospitality was warm and welcomed, especially after such a long journey. This was the one place where we could put the cares of the world behind us, for at least a few days. It was our home away from home, truly a place of rest.

The house was filled to capacity with my parents, three siblings, a brother-in-law, a niece, and a nephew. Our days together were filled with many different meals, including turkey, ham, and rouladen. There were far too many desserts and homemade treats to list them all. We would all play outside, tobogganing on Grandpa's hill, as long as weather permitted. The ladies would play Scrabble with Grandma, while the guys would play Blades of Steel, a video game. We sipped our coffee over many conversations, catching up on each other's lives.

One evening, as we sat around the sunken living room, with the fireplace crackling, I suggested, "Why don't we go around and each share something we are thankful for?" After all, 1 Thessalonians 5:18 says, "*Give thanks in all circumstances; for this is God's will for you in Christ Jesus.*"

This particular Christmas, I was struck by how much grace I had been living under, over the past few years. God's grace had enabled me to not burn out while attending to our young son's disabilities.

Dylan was five years old and had finally taken some steps this past year. I was the one who was with him the most during a typical day. Although at times I was overwhelmed with meeting his needs on top of the rest of the family's needs, most of the time it was very doable. Looking back, I realized that I'd rarely felt fatigue. God was allowing me to see how His grace was carrying me in the day to day.

With this in mind, it was easy for me when my turn came, to share this revelation with my family. I was so thankful for this gift God was reminding me of. The posture of my heart in giving thanks was a powerful way to end the year. I am reminded each Christmas of this story and ponder what I am thankful for as each year comes to a close.

Christmas Chaos

by

Sandra Lammers

We finally had to have our faithful companion and friend, Sasha, put down. It was a hard and emotional time for both my husband and me. Nonetheless, with Christmas just around the corner, we were expecting to enjoy the birth of Christ and all the festivities. I pulled out the decorations and decked the halls. I had the carpet shampooed, and cleaned the yard from the former barrage of doggie bombs. For the first time in a long time—we were also empty nesters—I had nothing to tie me down at home. One morning I sat there looking at my perfectly clean house with the quietness—which most people only dream about—surrounding me. Everything was perfect; too perfect.

Before I could catch and harness it, the thought popped into my head we need a little chaos in our lives. Too late—I had put it out there. I have no idea why God considers a little quickie thought a serious prayer, and sometimes seems to ignore those long drawn-out intercessory ones. He's God, however, and our Father knows best.

A few days before Christmas our dear daughter-in-law, Paige, was visiting an online site advertising fur babies for sale. In one of the ads, there was a picture of two nearly identical female Boxer and Ridgeback cross pups for sale.

We went to see them—just to look, of course. After all we weren't looking for a puppy. Maybe one that was already house broken, but a puppy? How on earth, with my limited mobility—I have Parkinson's—and Mark being so busy, were we going to train a puppy?

Well, you all know how that goes. One cuddle and face wash later and we were hooked. The clincher was that the one we chose was named Sasha. Writing on the wall? Perhaps. On Christmas Eve we brought our new wriggly bundle home with us. We renamed her Abby.

The next few weeks were a bit of a blur—with doggy potty training, and loss of sleep for us—as we dealt with the insecurities that a new puppy goes through. I felt like a new mom but without the hormones. Thankfully, Mark had some time off over the holidays. Abby was so fast it took both of us to keep the Christmas tree unscathed. Even a very large barricade of plywood didn't keep her out of the living room. She would jump right over it and keep going just like one of those super-duper bouncy balls that go everywhere.

There were times when I thought we were crazy to be doing this. However, we had a hard time staying angry as we gazed at such a cute, intelligent face, even when Abby had my good slipper hanging from her mouth. As I stared at my puppy pee-stained carpet and heard those oversized paws gallop across the kitchen floor I couldn't help but giggle. I hope Paige knows how much joy this little bit of chaos with legs brought into our lives.

It was the perfect Christmas. Not because every-thing was neat and orderly and well planned. It was perfect because of the love-filled confusion and disorder that this furry gift brought into our lives. We have so many self-imposed expectations that we put on ourselves. Maybe we could all use a little bit of chaos to remind us of the real reason that we celebrate Christmas.

"Our mouths were filled with laughter, our tongues with songs of joy" (Psalm 126:2).

That Special Day

by

L. Marie Enns

Christmas has always been special. I don't remember exactly when I first heard the story of the baby in a manger, the angels, and the shepherds. It seems that I have always known it, but when I was little, I didn't understand the significance of it.

Our family lived in a community of homesteaders in a wooded area of Saskatchewan. A few days before Christmas, Dad searched and found a spruce small enough to set up in the house for our Christmas tree. We kids helped Mom decorate it.

Christmas was the only day of the year that I awoke early, because I was so excited about the gifts I would receive. I couldn't wait to hear Dad stoking the fire in the heater, signalling that, at last, we could get up. Northern winter mornings were dark, and it was hard to guess what time it was. The waiting seemed much longer than it really was. Once I knew Dad was up, I hurried downstairs to find my plate of candy and nuts, with my wrapped gifts placed beside it. It was a Mennonite custom for children to set plates or bowls at their places on the table on Christmas Eve to get their treats and gifts.

The gifts we received were neither expensive nor extraordinary; but because we didn't have much, we appreciated simple things when we received them. In the 1930s and even 1940s, we had the basic food, clothing, and shelter. However, cash for extras, such as

104

toys and candy, was scarce. So we were thrilled with our presents of colouring books and crayons, books of paper dolls with changeable wardrobes, storybooks, and simple table games. In more prosperous years, girls might receive dolls, and boys might get Meccano® sets.

We lit the candles on our tree on Christmas morning when it was still rather dark, and their light made the tinsel sparkle. After opening gifts, singing "Silent Night" near the candle-lit tree, and having breakfast, we travelled via horse-and-sleigh to the Christmas service in our log church building. We children asked each other, "What did you get?"

Then we settled down to sing the carols while one of the women played the old pump organ. After that we listened to the preacher telling about the baby Jesus in the manger and the angels announcing the good news to the shepherds, or some other aspect of the Christmas story. After the closing song and prayer, we went home or to my aunt and uncle's house and had dinner together.

When still quite young, perhaps preschool or primary school age, I heard that Jesus will return some day to take His followers to Heaven. I thought that would be good, but I hoped He wouldn't come before Christmas! Years later, I understood that if I was enjoying the wonders of Heaven, I would never miss my little earthly gifts.

Every year we prepared for a Christmas concert at school and another at church. What joy it was to learn and sing the carols. As I grew older I sang in women's trios, mixed quartets, and in church, school, and community choirs. I also enjoyed singing solo renditions of "O Holy Night" and "Gesù Bambino."

While I was attending Teachers' College in Saskatoon, my brother, who was studying medicine in Winnipeg, came to Saskatoon and took me to hear Handel's Messiah before we bussed home together to Meadow Lake for Christmas. The performance was held in Third Avenue United Church, which has wonderful acoustics. I had never experienced anything so rapturous before. Years later I was privileged to hear Messiah again in that same old church and once again it was awesome. The only thing I could have enjoyed even more would have been to sing with that choir myself. The closest I ever got was an opportunity to sing the "Hallelujah Chorus" with a choir.

While teaching Primary music, the highlight of the year for me was Christmas time when I taught the children carols. I enjoyed hearing those clear, young voices sing at the program.

On most Christmases I sang at some function or another. Now age has crept up on me and I am fortunate if I can go and listen to a program, let alone have any part in the performance. I can still sing, but walking and standing with a cane and having arthritic pain makes it awkward.

Christmas has also been important in my writing. I have written more pieces about this season than on any other topic. I like to include a new poem or devotional with my Christmas letter. I enjoy exchanging greetings with relatives and friends, many of whom I may hear from only once a year.

At Christmas, it has been fun to watch my children, and then later, my grandchildren, enjoy their new toys. It has helped my joy of giving to increase and my joy of getting to decrease.

We seldom get our whole family together for Christmas. Sometimes we go to their homes in Chicago, Fort Chipewyan, Abbotsford, or North Saanich; and other times, some come home. Occasionally we have gone carolling, and we like to attend special concerts if they are available where we are. We usually still sing "Silent Night" on Christmas morning, just like we did long ago on the homestead.

As I matured, I began to realize what the Christmas story is really about. I learned that Jesus didn't originate as a baby, but He had been with His heavenly Father from the beginning. Then He took on the form of a baby to become human as well as divine so He could die on the cross to pay for all our sins. God, in His love for us, graciously sent His Son to free us from sin so that, through faith in Him, we can become children of God and have everlasting life (John 3:16). Now Christmas holds a much deeper meaning, as I understand how it relates to the events of Good Friday and Easter.

I still enjoy receiving presents, but they aren't as important or exciting anymore. (Now I can sleep in Christmas morning too!) I am much more grateful for the gift of salvation and eternal life, and the love, peace, and joy that Jesus gives. God's gift to us is what, most of all, makes Christmas special!

Want to keep Christ in Christmas?

*Feed the hungry, clothe the naked,
forgive the guilty, welcome the unwanted,
care for the ill, love your enemies,
and do unto others as you would
have done unto you.*

- Steve Maraboli

REFLECTIONS & DEVOTIONS

What Were They Thinking?

by

Carol Schafer

What were they thinking? Those sage souls who travelled from afar, somewhere called The East? Those wise in their own ancient ways and understandings, but with enough scholarly curiosity to gaze upon the heavens night after night, straining to discern whether the heavens might be declaring something greater.

What were they thinking as they gathered together to discuss and debate? As they leaned in and shifted elbows around a fine table with burnished, exotically scented oil lamps whose flames cast swaying shadows across their faces. Brows furrowed, discussions muted, debates rising, minds caught in desperate cravings to know the wanderings of the galaxies. Theory and speculation. Sky maps and old writings. For what purpose did their lives converge only to propel them on a quest they could neither comprehend nor deny?

What were they thinking when asked for reasons for the unreasonable-seeming journey? Did they dare cautious divulgence? Or guard the mysteries in securely wrapped cloaks of silence, hidden in that place where unspoken matters remain secrets?

What were they thinking when servants informed them that all was ready? In order. The journey to begin the moment the heavens assented. The provisions, the maps, the coins—all packed, ready for loading when the final instruction was spoken.

What were they thinking when bidding farewell to

those they loved but would leave behind for the sake of the quest? I love you but the quest demands this of me. I love you but I must know the answer, the truth. I love you but the choice before me leaves me no choice. I love you but I cannot truly live without knowing the Ruler who is to be greater than all of these.

What were they thinking when their caravan camped under the heavenly canopy that first night? The second? The fortieth? Did they rest by day and travel by night through unfamiliar surroundings lit by holy light? Their attentions illuminated by new thoughts, as a wandering itinerary guided by a sole brilliance drew them in and to and through great and mysterious wonderings.

What were they thinking when huddled around the night fires? Whisperings, glances, unspoken understandings bonding their truth-parched souls as they raised goatskins of cool water to their cracked lips. Or perhaps fears and fierce arguments voiced and resolved in barely heard whispers. Did they question the quest? Consider turning back? Discuss the dangers? Divert their course to shadow their purpose? Or steadfastly determine that pressing on was the only option?

What were they thinking as they passed by fields and groves and villages? A furtive glance taking in everything without even a tilt of gaze or a turn of head. To be "other" than those who stared. To be the spectacle, or, possibly, the target.

What were they thinking while gazing upward still at the faithful light that had drawn them this far? Far from home and the ancient understandings of the order of things. On the precipice of all that was yet to unfold and would forever alter all they knew. Such long years of hopes and fears. Perhaps unbidden tears. Of weariness or joy? Lamentation or expectation? Fulfillment so near and yet, not yet?

What were they thinking as they ascended to the

holy city not their own? What squint of the eyes relieved the glare of reflected sunlight against the limestone edifices defying the burning heat of clear sky? What misgivings itched in the back of their minds? What soreness of thought outmatched the soreness of body after all those camel-jostled weeks?

What were they thinking when standing before the seated tyrant-king? That unholy scowler plying them with questions and more questions. The false arch of eyebrow, the feigned loyalty to another, the deadly command. What trepidation assailed as they struggled to hold countenances unreadable? The pure and holy quest assaulted by the evil intent of one so-called "The Great." The evil tyrant occupying a throne not truly his own. What words slipped their guard, nearly aborting their quest? Endangering the One whose heart pulsed with truly royal blood.

What were they thinking as relief swept them beyond the city walls? As they brought out common robes to shelter from stares and recognition until darkness could cover them with a generous measure of anonymity among the cloak-headed masses.

What were they thinking when, later, the object of their search was found? A babe? An innocent babe in a world ridden with hatred and greed and pain. A babe whose star had brought them to this humble place. The girl-mother with the gentle eyes and the sad-proud smile. The husband who stood his earthly ground by her side. The babe who slept in peace reminiscent of Heaven. A babe declared by the heavens. A babe like and yet so unlike any other. A babe to be revered. Worshipped. Served. And loved. Forever.

What were they thinking? Those wise men of old as they fell down and worshipped Him. He who had claimed their lives and allegiance. Who had called them unto Himself through His very own creation.

What were they thinking?

No Gravy For Christmas
by
Tracy Krauss

The kitchen was filled with the savoury aroma of Christmas dinner. My daughters were bustling about getting the food on the table while my husband finished carving the turkey. I was busy stirring the gravy. It had thickened beautifully and was a rich golden colour. All it needed was a pinch of seasoning. As good-natured banter flew about the room, I reached for the salt shaker, undid the cap, and began to shake—and dumped the entire contents into the gravy!

Why would anyone take the cap off of the salt shaker? This was the million-dollar question for which I had no answer. It was just one of those absent-minded things—one little mistake that ruined the whole batch. We ate Christmas dinner minus gravy that year.

Although the incident didn't ruin Christmas entirely, I was quite upset that I had done such a silly thing. The family were all very forgiving, even though I felt terrible. In the end, we enjoyed the meal and the rest of the festivities continued, gravy or no gravy.

It reminded me of life in general. Sometimes when we mess up, no amount of apologizing will change the consequences of our actions. Yet, God, in His forgiveness, encourages us to carry on and things usually turn out in the end. No matter what the disaster, there is reassurance that God is in control.

"Blessed is the one whose transgressions are forgiven, whose sins are covered. Blessed is the one whose sin the Lord does not count against them and in whose spirit is no deceit" (Psalm 32:1-2).

113

A Place of Refreshing
by
Sandra Somers

Christmas is supposed to be the most wonderful time of the year, but sometimes it isn't so wonderful when we experience heartache, loss of loved ones, or emptiness.

There was one year in particular when I was lonely leading up to Christmas. Within a period of six weeks, three significant people were swept out of my life. My room-mate of six years had just bought a house and I decided not to move in with her, knowing I would be buying my own house in the next few months. One of my best friends was about to leave to teach in a mission school in the Philippines. And a good male friend chose to drop out of my life.

To help fill the void, I asked my young nephews, Cory, who was six, and Drew, four, to help decorate my Christmas tree. The boys took out the decorations from my box and spread them on the floor. While I was attaching the lights and checking to see that they were artistically arranged, my nephews quietly played with the gold garlands and unbreakable ornaments.

It was an adventure for all of us to place the ornaments in the best spots, and my nephews draped the garlands just like their mom did on her tree. All the while I thought how unique it was to have two small boys decorate with me.

After we finished, Cory brought out a roll of papers tied carefully with a silver ribbon. As he knelt to place it under the tree, he said, "I have a gift for you. I made it at school." I hadn't even noticed that he brought it! It was my first Christmas gift that year.

Later, when I unwrapped Cory's gift, I discovered a series of Christmas activities that only a child in Grade One would have made—dot-to-dot, pictures of Santa and his elves, and addition and subtraction exercises.

I was touched by Cory's thoughtfulness. Little did he know how much his gift meant to his lonely aunt!

I saw the Lord that Christmas, and I became especially aware that God is waiting to sweep into the vacuum of our lives and refresh us with others' love and caring.

"What joy for those whose strength comes from the Lord," the Psalmist wrote, *"...When they walk through the Valley of Weeping, it will become a place of refreshing springs"* *(Psalm 84:5-6, NLT).*

A Plate Full of Hope at Christmas

by

Bob Jones

My friend Kathy Kapteyn was dealing with her recent diagnosis of cancer at the same time as her mom endured cancer treatments one province away. When someone is facing the effects of two cancers, one needs all the help one can get. So when Kathy texted me a picture of a license plate with a special message, I was grateful she was encouraged.

Chemotherapy and radiation treatments had left Kathy suffering from severe nausea, exhaustion, and unease. A few days earlier, her husband's truck had been stolen from their driveway. Life was piling on.

Kathy knew she was in good hands with the medical personnel at the Cross Cancer Institute in Edmonton, Alberta. What she wanted was the assurance that she was safe in God's hands and He would see her through.

On the way to a radiation treatment on December 23, 2014, she and her husband Jim found themselves driving behind a Chevrolet Avalanche. The owner had a vanity plate that displayed five simple letters — "U" "L" "B" "O" "K."

A creative arrangement of the letters conveyed a timely message leaving Kathy momentarily speechless. If you know Kathy, you'd have to call that a miracle in itself. The real miracle was the message of the licence plate— "UL B OK."

What are the odds of a cancer patient asking

116

God for help, driving behind a vehicle with a license plate declaring, "You'll be OK?" Kathy had her early Christmas present, the reassurance she was looking for, from the God of perfect timing.

In his book, *Divine Alignment*, Squire Rushnell calls experiences like this "godwinks"—events that make you think, *What are the odds of that?* They are reminders that God has His eye and His hand on you.

God would later direct Kathy's attention to the verse of the day in her Bible reading app—*Isaiah 41:10. "So do not fear, for I am with you; do not be dismayed for I am your God. I will strengthen you and help you; I will uphold you with my righteous right hand."*

On May 6, 2015, Kathy's oncologist told her the chemo and radiation treatments had worked—she was cancer free—a final reassurance that God safely had her in His hands.

Needing assurance from the Lord? Ask away, and then watch for your own "godwinks."

Redeeming the Season
by
Kimberley Payne

Christmas Day depressed me. After all the hype and excitement leading up to December twenty-fifth, I always felt let down and depleted.

Don't get me wrong. I loved to unpack my gifts and watch the joy on my kids' faces as they tore open their presents. But after the rush of fun, I inevitably felt empty. I found myself feeling down in the dumps and dragging for the rest of the day. Until the year I turned thirty-five.

That year, I decided something had to change. I didn't want Christmas to be about just one day. I didn't want to set my sights on only twenty-four hours. I needed an attitude change.

To start with, I decided to celebrate the entire Christmas season. Maybe others were already doing this, but up to this time, I had always focussed on getting to December 25th. Now I planned to enjoy each day as a celebration of the season.

It wasn't a huge change, but rather a shift in my thought process. Instead of opening each day on the advent calendar as another day closer to Christmas, I reflected on and celebrated each day in and of itself.

I began to put into action those words, "Remember the reason for the season." I thanked God for the season, recognizing that my heart needn't think about the birth of Christ as a one-day event, but as something that affects my every day.

I realized that a gift doesn't have to be something

physical or something wrapped. I could give the gift of my time and volunteer to help at my children's school or at my church. To give the gift of encouragement, I could thank the women who decorated the church for the holidays, or call a friend I hadn't talked to in years.

I could extend the season by putting up my Christmas lights at Halloween to give the children a pretty alternative to all the ugliness and fear of that night. And I could leave them up until the end of February. The winter months can be depressing, and this would be just one small way I could bring the joy of Christmas forward.

Instead of sending out Christmas cards, I could make an effort to send out cards on any occasion, through-out the year. In our techno-savvy world, it feels nice to receive a handwritten card in the mail.

Now Christmas Day no longer depresses me. Yes, it is the time to celebrate the birth of our Lord and Saviour Jesus Christ; but it's worth celebrating 365 days of the year.

An Encounter with Jesus
by
Steph Beth Nickel

"When they had seen him, they spread the word concerning what had been told them about this child, and all who heard it were amazed at what the shepherds said to them. But Mary treasured up all these things and pondered them in her heart. The shepherds returned, glorifying and praising God for all the things they had heard and seen, which were just as they had been told" (Luke 2:17-20).

Picture the scene with me.

It's like any other night out in the fields near Bethlehem. The shepherds are tending their flocks, protecting them from predators, making sure none of them wander away.

But then something amazing happens, something not one of them expects: an angel appears in the sky above them.

An angel? But we're just shepherds. No one pays attention to us.

But that angel proclaims the Good News to these shepherds. And just when they think the night can't get any more unbelievable, it does. This heavenly messenger is joined by vast numbers of his fellow angels.

"'Glory to God in the highest heaven, and on earth peace to those on whom his favour rests,' they declared" (Luke 2:14).

After the heavenly host disappears and the night sky is

once again dotted with thousands of stars, the shepherds determine to go in search of the Newborn the angels spoke of.

There is no indication that they worry about who
will take care of the sheep or how strange a procession of
shepherds will look making their way through the streets
of the now-overcrowded town of Bethlehem. They simply
have to see for themselves.

And when they do...

This is one of my favourite portions of scripture.

These uneducated, unrespected, ordinary men,

"spread the word concerning what had been told them" (Luke 2:17).

They can't help it.

And as they make their way back to their flocks,

*"the shepherds [return], glorifying and praising God for all
the things they had heard and seen, which were just as they
had been told" (Luke 2:20).*

Have you encountered the Saviour?

How did you respond?

Like the shepherds, will you—will I—spread the word?

Will we go on our way "glorifying and praising God?"

Pray with me: Lord God, thank You for making
Yourself known to ordinary men and women. May we
never become so preoccupied with our busyness or the
familiarity of the Christmas story that we don't marvel
at the wonder of that first Christmas night. May we,
like the shepherds, make every effort to come into Your
presence. May we be willing to set aside our everyday
responsibilities in order to do so. And then, after we've
spent time with You, may we go on our way, glorifying and
praising You and making known what we've learned. In
Jesus' name. Amen.

The Most Important Thing
by
Sally Meadows

It's always hard saying goodbye to my son after the Christmas holidays are over, when he returns to university several provinces away. As his departure date approached this particular year, I wondered where the time had gone.

As a home-based entrepreneur, I often find it hard to draw boundaries between my work and personal life, and more so this year with deadlines looming. I had taken a few days off before and after Christmas Day, and had squeezed in as much work as possible when my late-rising son was sleeping, or out reacquainting himself with the city. But did I spend *enough* time with him? He visits only twice a year, and although he is an adult, I still question whether I fall short as a parent.

Driving my son to the airport, I asked him what the highlights of this Christmas season were for him. Did he enjoy himself? Was he happy with his holiday? And the dreaded question: Did we spend enough time together? He didn't answer right away. Then, thoughtfully, he said:

"Although what I did with Dad was more fun—eating out, working out together, and seeing the jazz band—I really appreciated the time you spent with me. You helped me. For me, that's the most important thing."

Reflecting back on our quiet conversations in the glow of the Christmas tree lights, it took all my strength not to tear up right then and there. My son has a disability that can make it difficult for him to communicate his emotions. I have come to accept that he might not thank me, or express sadness, when he leaves. But this…this was a Christmas time treasure I will remember for a long time. He couldn't have been clearer in letting me know that the time we spent together this December, as we talked through and sought solutions for challenges with university and life in general… well, it mattered to him.

As I watched my son shuffle through the airport security queue until I could no longer see his slight frame, tears threatened to spill once again. But as I walked back through the airport terminal to the parking lot, the joy singing in my heart trumped any sadness. There is nothing more wonderful than knowing that I have made a difference in the life of a loved one.

And perhaps next Christmas, we'll work on adding in some fun, too!

"Start children off on the way they should go, and even when they are old they will not turn from it" (Proverbs 22:6).

The Old is Made New Again

by

Lynne Collier

As I wondered how to dispose of the dead vines I'd gathered in the fall from the trees in our backyard, I wrapped one around my arm to carry it to the fire pit. By the time I got there I had a thick circle of dried vine and the makings of a lovely Christmas wreath. The dead and withered vine, which was choking our trees and therefore destined for the fire, suddenly had a new life and a new, more beautiful purpose. I could take the old vine and make useful Christmas decorations. I made three wreaths that year, one for myself and one each for my two daughters. They looked delightful wrapped in tartan ribbon and tied in a bow with leaves from our evergreen trees.

In 2 Corinthians, God tells us that He reconciled Himself to the world through the death and resurrection of His Son, Jesus Christ. God no longer counts our sins against us. If we are in Christ we are a new creation. The old person is dead to sin and the new person is alive in Christ. We too, have a new life and a new, more beautiful purpose.

"Therefore, if anyone is in Christ, the new creation has come: The old has gone, the new is here!" (2 Corinthians 5:17).

Do you feel like a new creation? If not, ask God to reveal Himself to you as you walk with Him today. What old things do you see that are made new? Do you see old rusted watering cans painted in bright colours, adorning someone's garden? Or, maybe, an old lamp stand with a colourful bowl repurposed as a birdbath? If we can transform old things, which seem of little worth, how much more can our loving God transform us?

Pray with me: Heavenly Father, transform me into the image of my Lord and Saviour, Jesus Christ, Your Son. Show me that I am a new person because of Him.

For further reading, see 2 Corinthians 5:11-21.

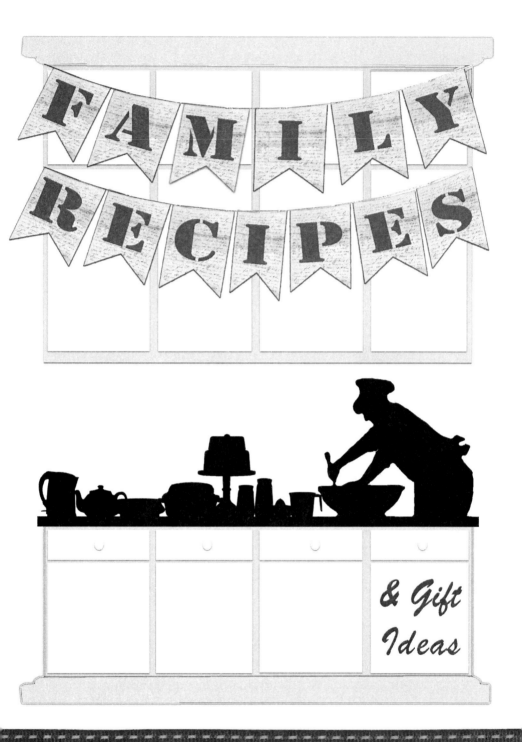

FAMILY RECIPES

& Gift
Ideas

Don't Mess with the Stuffing
by
Brenda C Leyland

In our family, it's always been called "stuffing." Everybody we knew called it that, even our cousins. One Christmas at Aunty and Uncle's place, while sitting at the kids' table, my little sister, older cousin, and I thought ourselves most clever to pronounce that we were stuffing ourselves with stuffing. All through dinner we giggled at our little joke, filling our faces with the savoury dish till indeed we were stuffed.

Even back then, stuffing was the favourite part of our Christmas dinner. Although we like turkey, it is, as my sister recently pointed out, merely the conduit for this seasoned, bready concoction.

As Mom prepared the bird and stuffing Christmas morning, she would try to shoo everyone out of the kitchen so she could chop and sauté in peace. There was no chance of that: my siblings and I, and sometimes even our Dad, would jostle for position to watch (more like sneak finger-fuls of) the savoury ingredients mounting up in the big bowl. Mom would mildly scold us to get our hands "out of there." That first whiff of sizzling onions and celery would always set our mouths watering.

Mom, as a young wife, developed her own recipe for stuffing, distinct from that of her own mother, who always diced in turkey giblets. Instead, browned ground beef and finely diced ham replaced the offending viscera.

Years later, it was my turn to host Christmas dinner.

As a young woman, I was eager to try new stuffing recipes, and I found some interesting ones in *Ladies Home Journal* and *Canadian Living* magazines, which suggested adding sausage, apple, and sage, or chestnuts and dried fruit. That experiment and any future ones did not go over well, for someone at the table invariably moaned about the lack of "real" stuffing.

In the end, we all agreed. No more experimenting, just make my mother's traditional, tried and true recipe. For more than half a century, it's been making our family happy. Whoever is hosting welcomes suggestions to adjust anything on the Christmas dinner menu, but please don't mess with the stuffing.

Mom's Christmas Stuffing

2 large loaves white bread, day old (about 900 g)
1½ medium onions, diced
3 to 4 celery ribs, diced
2 cups finely chopped, cooked ham
¼ to ½ cup butter, for sautéing onions, celery, and ham
1½ pounds lean ground beef (about 700 g)
cooking oil (as needed)
1 to 2 tsp poultry seasoning—start with 1 tsp and adjust to taste
1 tsp salt—to taste
½ tsp freshly ground pepper—to taste
1¾ to 2 cups low salt chicken broth
1/3 cup butter, melted, for pouring over stuffing before baking

1. One to two days prior to turkey day, cube bread and set out on cookie sheets to thoroughly dry. Toss once or twice so that all sides get exposure. When dry and no longer soft to the touch, set aside in a very large bowl and cover with a clean tea towel.

2. In a large skillet, melt ¼ to ½ cup butter. Gently sauté onions and celery until soft. Add chopped ham and sauté for a few minutes. Remove from pan and set aside in a bowl.

3. In the same skillet, add (if needed) some cooking oil. Brown the ground beef; break up the meat as it browns. Dust with salt, pepper, and poultry seasoning.

4. Add the sautéed onion mixture to the browned beef.

5. Sprinkle on the measured poultry seasoning, salt, and pepper. Mix together.

6. Bring out bowl with bread cubes. Sprinkle chicken broth over cubes to lightly moisten. Add onion and meat mixture. Stir everything together.

7. Carefully adjust seasonings to taste—poultry seasoning can overpower. Add chicken broth if bread is still dry; the mixture should cling together somewhat, but not so it's drippy-wet.

8. Put the stuffing into a large buttered roaster or casserole dish. Pour the melted butter over the stuffing; this will bring out the flavour and help keep it from drying out.

9. Cover and put in a preheated 190°C (375°F) oven for about 30 minutes or until heated through. Stir at least once, preferably around the 15-minute point.

Serves 10 with leftovers.

Note: It's only once a year, so we don't fuss about calories.

How to Eat Leftover Stuffing
1. Layer with turkey slices and cranberries in a sandwich.
2. Reheat with lots of gravy over top.
3. My personal favourite: cold, straight from the bowl in the refrigerator, with a fork. Warning: this last one often means fending off other forks aiming for the same snack.

Grannie's Easy Fudge
by
Carol Elaine Harrison

The shallow, hexagon-shaped tin with its lacy swirls surrounding the image of a nineteenth century couple meant Grannie had made fudge for Christmas. It sat unopened as we ate our meal of turkey with all the traditional trimmings, did the dishes, and opened our presents. By mid-afternoon the wooden nut bowl with its nutcrackers and picks, a variety of chocolates, and hard candy graced the table. Finally, Grannie removed the lid from the old tin and cut the home-made fudge into bite-size pieces. The milk chocolate sweetness melted in my mouth. My mother's admonition, "I think you've had enough for now," always happened before I finished enjoying my fill of the Christmas treat.

As my grandmother advanced in years, the venue for Christmas gatherings changed to my parent's home, but Grannie always arrived with one or two tins. She handed them off with these words, "I don't know if anyone still wants my fudge but decided to make it anyway." We would smile and anticipate the time we could indulge in her delicious treat.

In time, Grannie shared her easy fudge recipe with me so I could carry on the tradition. I became the one to bring a tin filled with milk chocolate fudge, adding a butter-scotch variety in a second tin. The old tins, lined with wax paper, have been replaced with plastic containers. The use of a microwave has simplified the process. Yet the taste remains the same, stirring up my childhood memories.

I have taught some of my grandchildren to make

this recipe and we have experimented with multiple varieties. It is an easy-to-make but tasty treat for family gatherings, to give as gifts, or to take to holiday potlucks.

Grannie's Easy Fudge

½ cup margarine or butter
¼ cup canned milk (evaporated)
1 small (270 g) package chocolate chips
2 cups icing sugar

Melt margarine or butter. Add chocolate chips, canned milk, and icing sugar. Stir; then heat in a microwave safe bowl for 2-3 minutes. Beat with a mixer until smooth and creamy. Put in a greased pan, waxed paper lined tin, or plastic dish 22 cm X 16.5 cm X 5 cm (8 ½ in X 6 ½ in X 2 in). For best results, place in the refrigerator until hardened. Here are some variations.

Butterscotch: use butterscotch chips in place of chocolate chips.
Raspberry chocolate: add a few drops of good quality raspberry flavouring to dark or milk chocolate chips.
Orange chocolate: add a few drops of good quality orange flavouring to dark or milk chocolate chips.
Cookies & cream: use one-and-a-half packages (225 g per package) of white chocolate chips. After beating the mixture add ½ to ¾ cup of crushed Oreo cookies.
Mint: add a few drops of good quality mint flavouring to dark or milk chocolate chips.
Peanut butter: make a white or milk chocolate fudge. Immediately, in a separate bowl take ¼ cup of peanut butter chips, add a bit of canned milk, and melt in the microwave. Beat by hand then drop by the spoonful into the chocolate mixture in the pan. Then swirl like you would do for a marble cake.

For other variations, use your imagination and have fun experimenting. Maybe this will become a family tradition for you too.

Auntie Evie's "Kringle" Cookies
by
Sally Meadows

My mother's older sister, Evelyn, never had children of her own, but she was like a second mother to me. Despite living several provinces away as a single career woman, and later in New Jersey after she married my American uncle, she made it a point to visit my family whenever she could.

Almost every photo of my auntie and me shows her hugging and kissing me. We had a special relationship that I will never forget.

Besides the love of Jesus that exuded through her, my auntie was a wonderful homemaker. She was an excellent baker, and we always looked forward to the Christmas "Kringle" cookies that she brought with her whenever she visited, no matter what time of year it was.

As time went on and it became more difficult for my aunt to travel, she gave the recipe to my mother so that we could make our own cookies at Christmas. It became a treasured mother-daughter tradition, and one that I continued with my own children, in time.

Life took a detour when my aunt developed Alzheimer's in her seventies. I am grateful that my uncle brought her to meet my children before complications of this dreaded disease rendered her unable to travel. On her final visit before she passed away, despite her challenges in remembering who I was, I could still see and feel her beautiful essence.

When I think of my auntie's "Kringle" cookies, it's

more than a longing to taste her delectable baking. They are a symbol of my very real memories of being comforted, loved, and made to feel special by a woman of noble character (Proverbs 31:10-31). May there be someone in your life who blesses you this way too.

*Auntie Evie's "Kringle" Cookies**

1 cup margarine or butter
¼ cup sugar
1 tsp vanilla
2 cups flour
1 cup chopped nuts
red and/or green decorator's sugar

Cream margarine (or butter) and sugar together. Add in vanilla. Add flour and nuts, and mix well. Shape tablespoonsful of dough into balls. Roll in green or red decorator sugar. Place balls on greased baking sheets. Bake at 150°C (300°F) for 25 to 30 minutes. Remove immediately onto a cooling rack.

Enjoy!

*Source unknown

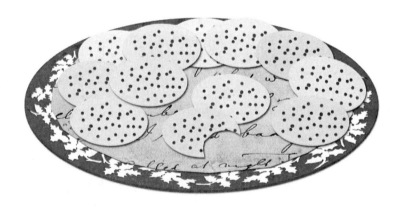

Of Popcorn Balls and Candy Bags

by

Sandra Somers

My mother's gift was serving, especially when it came to food. She loved making candy bags at Christmas, and popcorn balls were an integral part of this tradition.

One December afternoon when Mom was a child, she and her sister arrived home from school to the aroma of delicious caramel popcorn. In pioneer days, luxuries were scarce and her mother was strict, so the girls could eat only one popcorn ball each before Christmas Day.

When Mom began to make her own popcorn balls, she used her mother's recipe, one that had been handed down from neighbour to neighbour, going back a number of years.

Mom began to make candy bags for the Christmas program in her rural church when she was in her fifties. In the early days when the church was small, she made about twenty-five bags for the children. The congregation gradually grew, and in her last years, she made 150 bags, giving any that were left over to the adults.

Hers were candy bags of quality, and she took great care in selecting the contents. She started during the Halloween season, buying tiny chocolate bars and miniature Life Savers® rolls, later adding mandarin oranges and candy from a candy shop. Then in December, she made popcorn balls, placing them in a container to freeze until the day she packed the bags.

A day or two before the Christmas program, Mom was ready to fill the bags. She wrapped the popcorn balls in plastic wrap, a security against getting the contents

133

stuck together. Her large dining room table was covered with brown lunch bags, which looked like baby birds with mouths open ready to take the food the mother bird offered. Nothing pleased Mom more at the Christmas program than the neighbours praising her for such good candy bags. Some said they had never seen such quality.

As Mom entered her late eighties and early nineties, purchasing candy and assembling the bags became more challenging. I began buying the chocolate bars and drove her to the nearest Nutters store so she could choose individual candies. Other family members or neighbours helped fill the bags.

Mom made candy bags until she was ninety-two. By the next Christmas her health had failed, she was living in a seniors' lodge, and she was on kidney dialysis. The seniors at her church gathered to make the bags for her.

Mom passed away that winter. At her funeral, her church honoured her tradition by making candy bags for the extended family—minus the popcorn balls.

Mom had given this gift of service to her church for thirty-seven years.

Popcorn Balls

½ cup popcorn, unpopped
9 tbsp brown sugar
7 tbsp syrup
5 tbsp butter or margarine
1 tsp vanilla

1. Pop the popcorn and put in a large bowl. In a large pot, combine brown sugar, syrup, and butter or margarine. Stir well.
2. Bring mixture to a quick boil. Continue stirring. Boil until it reaches a soft ball stage (112° to 114°C; 234° to 238°F). Take pot off stove and add vanilla. Beat about 20 strokes.
3. Pour mixture over popcorn and mix well. Dip hands in cold water to keep the mixture from sticking before shaping mixture into small balls.

These popcorn balls freeze well.

Stef's Gingerbread Cookies

by

Charleen Raschke

¾ cup butter
¾ cup sugar
¾ cup molasses
¼ cup water
½ tsp salt
½ tsp baking soda
2 tsp ginger
2 tsp cinnamon
1 tsp nutmeg
¼ tsp allspice
½ tsp cardamom
3¼ cups flour

Cream butter and sugar until fluffy. Stir in molasses and water. Slowly add dry ingredients to wet ingredients. Divide dough in half and flatten into discs or circles. Wrap each one in plastic wrap and chill overnight.

On a lightly floured surface, roll each disc to 6 mm (¼ in) thickness. Cut out with cookie cutter shapes and place 2.5 cm (1 in) apart on parchment paper lined cookie sheet. Bake 6-10 minutes at 170°C (325°F) or until firm but not brown.

Decorate and enjoy!

Aunty Mavis's Christmas Cake
by
Charleen Raschke

3 cups Sultana raisins
1½ cups Thompson raisins

Place raisins in a bowl and pour hot water over them to cover. Wait 10-15 minutes, then drain and squeeze out all of the water, using your hands.

Add:
450 g glazed fruit
2 containers (375 mL each) halved red cherries
1½ cups chopped dates
1 cup cran-raisins
1 tsp each vanilla & almond extracts
1 cup raspberry or strawberry jelly (not jello)
Zest of one lemon and one orange

Stir and leave on the counter overnight, covered with a clean tea towel.

Dry Ingredients:
1½ cups flour
1½ tsp baking soda
½ tsp nutmeg
½ tsp salt
2 tsp cinnamon
¼ tsp cloves
1½ tsp baking powder
1 tsp allspice
½ tsp ginger
2 cups chopped pecans

Mix together. Add ¼ of the dry ingredients into the fruit mixture.

> Mix:
> 6 beaten eggs
> ¼ cup molasses
> 1 cup butter
> 1 cup brown sugar

Mix into the remaining ¾ dry ingredients. Then add everything together. Split the mixture evenly in three loaf pans lined with parchment paper. Bake at 135°C (275°F) for about two hours.

Small Treasures at Christmas
by
Carol Schafer

Once in a while, even the most savvy gift giver can be stumped. Finding meaningful gifts takes a lot of time and thought, and, for most people, the weeks leading up to Christmas leave little room for either. Still, wouldn't it be nice to give something special, maybe even unique, to those you love?

Finding special gifts for relatives can be especially challenging as the years go by. Maybe you don't get together as often anymore. Maybe the family units have experienced struggles, or even breakdowns. Certainly, those once-little nieces and nephews whose eyes lit up at the sight of a Christmas tree grew up too quickly. Long gone are the days when teddy bears, action figures, puzzles, and even storybooks were their delight. Now what? Are gift cards and pricey electronics the only options for young adults? Not so!

Think closer to home. Think Christmases past. For that matter, think birthdays past, picnics past, and family reunions past. Now, remember that shoebox of unsorted photos that Grandma and Grandpa never got around to putting into albums? Remember how photographs were taken before the arrival of digital photography? Remember when getting film developed meant ordering doubles and triples of print photographs?

You've got a big gift-giving win just waiting to happen! With minimal cost, a little ingenuity, and generous lead time, you can reconnect the present generation with their own family's past, even as you remind them how much they're loved.

To get it done, break the project into these seven steps.

Step 1: Do a photo sort. How many nieces and nephews are in your family? Start an envelope with each of their names. If you have doubles or triples of prints, consider who appears in the photo. Older nieces and nephews tend to show up in more photos, so be especially careful to find special photos of the younger ones. If a grandparent or other family member has passed on, try to find a photo of each child with that person.

Step 2: Think cropping. Do you have a photo of Grandpa with several grand kids colouring Easter eggs? And you have two copies? Great. But look closer. Which child is sitting next to Grandpa? Are they having a little chat? Super. Can you count the candles on a birthday cake and figure out whose special day it was? Is Grandma holding a new baby in a hospital room? Are several people in the photo but two of them didn't photograph well? Was the angle bad and half the photo is the back of someone's head? Don't toss anything until you decide whether cropping might salvage that shot. You might have a great photo of auntie and two cousins if you crop out the background people at the restaurant and the fire extinguisher on the wall. But don't crop yet.

Step 3: Hunt for small frames. Jot down a few notes about your photo selections or take your envelopes with you when you go shopping. Try second-hand stores for frames with interesting shapes and sizes. Check the frames for chips and scratches or any missing parts before you buy them. They don't have to be perfect, but you don't want unpleasant surprises when you're putting things together. Don't try to get everything you need in your initial purchase, just get enough to give yourself a good start. Plan to come back or visit another second-hand store. Expand your frame collection with simple, inexpensive dollar store selections. If you're going to buy extras of anything, go for the smaller frames.

Step 4: Clean the frames that have been previously owned. Wash the glass. Wipe the decorative frame border if it isn't washable. Use sticky tape to clean off the velvet backs. Remove those gummy spots from price stickers. Use tiny screwdrivers to tighten the screws that hold the back in place. Chances are, your frames will look new again, but some will definitely look like they belong to a different decade, which is great because you are framing photos from the past.

Step 5: When you have a block of time, get out your frames and the envelopes of photos. Sort, sort, sort! See what combinations work and match the obvious choices. This step is time consuming, so aim to match at least one photo with a frame for each person on your list. You can always do more, but keeping things more or less even will help you move your project forward.

Step 6: Crop the photos carefully. The easiest way to figure out where to crop is to use the glass or clear plastic from the frame. Place it over the part of the photo you wish to keep. Using a ballpoint pen, trace around the edges of the glass or plastic. Crop the photo and set it in the frame. Remember that the frame opening will usually be slightly smaller than the glass or plastic you are using, so don't trace or crop until you're sure you'll be pleased with the result. You may have to switch frames to accommodate the cropped photos. Plan for more than one session to complete this part of the project, so keep things handy in a box or basket. Pick up more frames when you've exhausted your possibilities. If you can get three small photo treasures for each person on your list, you've done well. They won't take up a lot of room to display and they'll look great grouped together. You can always pick up small photo albums for any photos that didn't work out for framing that you still want to pass along.

Step 7: Get out the gift bags and tissue paper. Write a card or note to each person who will receive this extraordinarily personal gift of treasured memories. Remind them of the special times you shared and how much they were and are loved.

When I did this project for nieces and nephews, it caught them by complete surprise. They certainly didn't expect to receive framed photos of themselves as young children for Christmas. It was a lot of work to put together, but exclamations of "I remember that fort we made!" and "Hey, I'd forgotten we had tea parties with those old dishes" were reported back to me.

Grandma and Grandpa worked hard to make their grandchildren's visits special. Those days may be forever gone, but the memories are closer than you might think. It's always worth the effort to honour loved ones across generations—and keep the shared memories alive.

Isaiah 9:6

For to us a child is born,
to us a son is given,
and the government
will be on his shoulders.
And he will be called:
Wonderful Counselor,
Mighty God,
Everlasting Father,
Prince of Peace.

DRAMAS & READINGS

The Christmas Card

by

Terrie Todd

Dedicated to Bob Guenther & Liz Driedger.

CAST:
JOE, a crusty old man
PAM, his 30-year-old granddaughter (a chip off the old block)

PROPS: Two worn and mismatched chairs, afghans, etc. A small table with a land line phone, out of style lamp, handful of mail, a folding TV table, box or laundry basket with folded clothing, jar of soup, three muffins, an orange, tray, teapot, two mugs.

SCENE: Joe's living room. The phone rings and continues to ring as we see JOE shuffle in, muttering and grousing. He carries a handful of mail.

JOE: Hold onto yer shorts, I'm comin'. (*Picks up phone.*) Yeah? (*Pause.*) Speak up, I can't hear ya. You what? … No, do I sound like the lady of the house? … Victoria's Secret? Yeah, she could use a little perking up. She passed away in 1972. (*Doorbell rings.*) Well, I'm sorry too, now get off my phone. I'm waitin' for my granddaughter to call. (*He hangs up in a huff and shuffles to his chair, muttering.*) Daft.

PAM: (*From off.*) Grandpa? (*Enters, carrying box.*) Grandpa?

JOE: Didn't anybody teach you to knock first?

PAM: I rang the bell. Didn't you hear it?

JOE: It's broke.

PAM: I heard it ring, Grandpa. You should really keep your door locked.

JOE: Fiddlesticks. In my day we didn't even have locks. What'd ya bring me?

PAM: (*Unpacking box.*) One load of clean laundry … one jar of homemade soup … three bran muffins … and a Christmas orange.

JOE: Nuthin good, eh. (*He continues sorting his mail.*)

PAM: Nope. How did your checkup with the doctor go?

JOE: Fool doctor.

PAM: What did he say?

JOE: He said, "Your hearing's getting worse, Mr. Weiss, but I wouldn't worry about it."

PAM: What did you say?

JOE: I said, "If your hearing was getting worse, I wouldn't worry about it either."

PAM: Whatcha working on there?

JOE: Sortin' my mail.

PAM: You get so much mail you have to sort it?

JOE: It's Christmas, you ninny. (*JOE thoughtfully examines the last envelope and adds it to one of the sorted piles.*) See, this stack is from all the people who want to sell me hearing aids, as if I need 'em. In this stack are my bills. (*Picks one up.*) This one's a year old already. (*Hands it to PAM.*) Here, send it a birthday card, will ya? (*He laughs at his own joke.*) And these are Christmas cards.

PAM: Christmas cards? I never realized you had so many friends.

JOE: I haven't got an enemy in the world. Outlived every blamed one of 'em! (*He laughs again, slapping his thigh.*) Course I got friends. (*Sorting through envelopes.*) My chiropractor. My insurance man. Omega Funeral Home. McKenzie's Funeral Home. My fitness club.

PAM: (*Picking up card from fitness club.*) Since when do you belong to a fitness club?

JOE: Since last year when they sold me a lifetime membership for the same price as a one-year. Suckers figured I'd be kickin' the bucket in about ten minutes, but I showed 'em. (*Proud of himself.*) Heh heh.

PAM: So . . . how often do you actually go?

JOE: (*Puzzled.*) Go where?

(*PAM just shakes her head. JOE picks up an envelope and tries opening it, fumbling and muttering.*)

PAM: Yeah, you showed 'em, all right. Want some help with that?

146

JOE: No. Yer too snoopy. (*He struggles, then gets annoyed that PAM is just watching.*) What are you lookin' at? Here, make yourself useful. (*He hands her his "garbage pile."*) Go throw this junk away.

PAM: Fine. I'll go make tea.

(*She exits and JOE continues to open his mail in a comical fashion, shredding most of it beyond recognition.*)

PAM: (*Offstage.*) Michael just got his report card. He really improved in math this year. Last night I was helping him find the lowest common denominator.

JOE: Haven't they found that thing yet? They were lookin' fer it when I was a kid!

PAM: And he's taking French! He already knows how to say please and thank you.

JOE: That's more than he can say in English.

PAM: What could be more clever than speaking two languages?

JOE: Keeping your mouth shut in one.

PAM: (*She enters carrying tea tray. It still has the junk mail on it.*) Did I tell you Michael's going to be in the Christmas play at church?

JOE: Didn't anybody tell him play-actin' is just for girls and sissies?

PAM: No, and don't you dare tell him that either. He loves being on stage.

JOE: Must take after his great-great aunt Molly.

PAM: How's she doing, anyway?

(*JOE glares at her until the light dawns.*)

PAM: Aunt Molly died, didn't she? (*JOE rolls his eyes.*) I'm sorry, Grandpa… I have a hard time keeping track of all your siblings. There were an awful lot of them, you know.

JOE: Well, I'm the last one left. That shouldn't be too hard to remember.

PAM: Now, we both know that's not quite true, don't we? (*Pause.*) Grandpa?

JOE: (*Putting his hand to his ear.*) What's that?

PAM: How come you could hear me from the kitchen but you can't hear me when I mention Aunt Audrey?

JOE: Speak up, I can't hear ya.

PAM: Okay, I guess we're not going to go there today. Or any day, most likely.

JOE: (*Pauses while they pour tea.*) That car of yours runnin' good?

PAM: Yeah, it's a bit of a gas guzzler, but it's okay.

JOE: Well, I could guzzle a little gas myself in this cold. (*Pause.*) That husband of yours still breeding cattle?

PAM: No—

JOE: Guess they pretty much do that all by themselves, eh? (*Cracks himself up again.*)

PAM: Very funny. He sold the cattle last spring, remember?

JOE: (*They sit quietly sipping their tea.*) That sister of yours call lately?

PAM: Hmph. That'll be the day. Mrs. High-and-Mighty hasn't spoken to me since I didn't show up for her precious housewarming party. More like a "Come and See How Rich I Am" party if you ask me.

JOE: Well, she's the only sister ya got and they ain't makin' any more. And yer little niece, Janie—

PAM: Jenny.

JOE: Yeah, Jenny. She isn't even gonna know you anymore. Maybe you should just get off yer high horse and call her first.

PAM: Oh, look who's talking! Maybe the day you call your sister, I'll think about calling mine.

JOE: It's not the same thing. I don't even know where Audrey is!

PAM: I thought we weren't going to talk about it.

JOE: Fine.

PAM: Fine. (*They drink their tea.*)

JOE: That house of yours stayin' warm enough?

PAM: Pretty much, yeah. (*Pause.*) Speaking of which, I need to pick Michael up from play practice and head home. We're putting up the tree tonight. Is there anything you need before I go?

JOE: Yeah. (*Pointing to junk mail.*) Throw that junk out like I told ya to.

PAM: Okay, okay. (*She picks it up.*) I put your soup in the fridge, you can just heat it in the microwave for—

JOE: Yeah, yeah, I heard ya.

PAM: And be sure to eat the bran muffins. They're good for your—

JOE: I know, I heard ya.

PAM: Okay. Well, bye then.

JOE: Bye. Tell Michael I'll come see his sissy play.

PAM: I will. (*She kisses the top of his head.*) Bye. (*She turns to go, sorting through his "junk mail." Suddenly stops.*) Oops. Grandpa, here's another Christmas card… you almost threw it out! (*She tries to hand it to him, but he ignores it.*)

JOE: Saw it already. Throw it out.

PAM: But, it's not even open—

JOE: Are you deaf? I said, throw it out!

PAM: Who do we know from Kitchener?

JOE: Give me that!

PAM: (*She opens it and gasps.*) Grandpa, it's from Aunt Audrey! You said you didn't know where she was!

JOE: Give me that, little miss snoopy pants.

(*PAM keeps it out of his reach.*)

PAM: (*Reading.*) "Dear Joe, I imagine you'll be pretty surprised to hear from me after all these years. It's Christmas time and I have good reason to believe it'll be my last on this earth. I have something important to say to you before I check out. I've been doing a lot of thinking and I realize I was such a fool to hold a grudge against you for so long. It certainly wasn't your fault if mother divvied things up unfairly. And anyways, it's just stuff. Letting stuff get in the way of a relationship with my own brother is just foolish. Please forgive me. If you can find it in your heart to patch things up, please call me at 519-555-2092. I would love to hear your voice one last time. Love, Audrey."

Grandpa, this is fantastic. She wants to make up! Give her a call.

(*JOE sits and folds his arms stubbornly across his chest.*)

PAM: Grandpa, come on. She's making the first move here.

(*No response.*)

PAM: Oh, I suppose you can't hear me again.

JOE: Mind yer own business. I ain't callin' nobody.

PAM: Well, then I will.

JOE: The heck you will.

PAM: She's my aunt, I can call her if I want. (*Picks up phone.*)

JOE: Not on my phone.

PAM: Fine. (*Hangs up, pulls a cell phone from her pocket and dials the number.*)

(*JOE acts mad but we can see he's curious.*)

PAM: Huh, that's funny. (*Dials again.*)

JOE: Fool woman probably gave me the wrong number just for spite.

PAM: Yes, information for Kitchener please. Do you have a listing for Audrey Weiss on 29th Street? I see. No, that's fine. Thank you very much. (*She puts phone back in her pocket and turns to go without a word.*)

(*JOE looks at her expectantly, but she says nothing. Finally, when she's almost out the door, he can't stand it.*)

JOE: Well?

PAM: Well, what?

JOE: Well, what did they say?

PAM: Thought ya didn't care.

(*He looks away stubbornly.*)

PAM: (*She sits, speaking gently.*) Grandpa, it looks like maybe you are the last one left in your family after all.

JOE: (*Turns to her slowly; we think he's going to soften.*) You mean she sent the card and then just dropped dead? She always was a nervy old crow.

PAM: (*Examining the card.*) I don't know. They said they don't have a listing under that name and the card makes it sound like she doesn't expect to be around much longer— (*Gasps.*) Oh, my goodness!

JOE: What?

PAM: (*Checking postmark.*) Grandpa, she mailed this in 2009!

JOE: Hmph! Shoulda used the pony express.

PAM: Don't you get it? This must have been sitting in some lost mail bin all this time!

JOE: (*Slowly he takes card from PAM and looks at it.*) Crazy old maid. Always did cheat at cards. (*He hands the card back to PAM.*) Ol' fool.

(*JOE turns to exit to the kitchen. He stops at the telephone, picks up the receiver, and hands it to PAM behind his back, without looking at her. She takes it. He exits. PAM watches him leave, then sits quietly for a moment, looking at the card and holding the receiver. She looks at the phone, finally dials and waits for an answer.*)

PAM: Hello? Jenny? Hi, sweetie, this is Aunty Pam. I'm good, how are you? It's so good to hear your voice! You're right, you haven't seen me in a long time, have you? Uh… is your mommy there? Yes. . .I'll wait.

(*Lights fade to black.*)

THE END

Gloria! A Christmas Play
by
Sharon Hamilton

CAST: Narrator, Zechariah*, Priest 1, Priest 2, Elizabeth*, Mary*, Mary's Mother, Joseph

Gabriel, Head angel, Singing angels, Dancing angels

Persons 1,2,3,4, Anna, Simeon

Shepherds, Sheep (*Parts suitable for young children.*)

People (*To sing in crowd scenes; can be extras or all actors not otherwise in scene.*)

* Solo singing parts.

PROPS: See individual scenes.

NARRATOR: "*Do not be afraid, for I am with you.*" God spoke these words many times before Jesus came. When Mary, an unmarried teenager, learned that she was going to be the mother of God's Son, she needed to know that God was near. Watch and see how many ways God reassures her and the people around her, starting with a priest named Zechariah.

Scene 1—Temple in Jerusalem
(*At rise: curtain, with opening into Holy of Holies, perpendicular to audience; incense container to left of curtain; Zechariah, Priest 1, Priest 2 holding three straws—standing to left of curtain. Gabriel hiding stage right. People to left of priests.*)

154

SONG: "O Come, O Come Emmanuel" (*Verse 1, sung by everyone on stage.*)

ZECHARIAH: We pray and pray for God to send the Messiah, but He hasn't. I prayed and prayed for God to send me a son, but He didn't.

PRIEST 1: God is faithful, Zechariah. He will answer our prayers in His own time.

ZECHARIAH: Yours, maybe. It's too late for me. (*They draw straws. Zechariah gets short one.*)

PRIEST 2: It's never too late to serve God. See? He chose you to burn incense.

(*Zechariah picks up incense container, goes through curtain and holds it up. Gabriel bursts out of hiding. Zechariah is afraid.*)

GABRIEL: Don't be afraid, Zechariah! God has heard your prayers. Your wife Elizabeth is going to have a son, and you must name him John. He will be like the prophet Elijah, and will get people ready for the Messiah.

ZECHARIAH: But my wife and I are both very old! How can I be sure this is going to happen?

GABRIEL: I am Gabriel, God's servant, and God sent me to tell you this good news. This is how you will know it is true: you will not be able to speak until your son is born. For God will make everything happen at the proper time. (*Exit.*)

(*Zechariah goes back through curtain to people.*)

PRIEST 1: What took you so long?
(*Zechariah tries to speak but can't. He holds his throat, then makes arm movements to show he has seen something tall.*)

PRIEST 2: There was somebody in there with you? He tried to choke you?
(*Zechariah shakes head then flaps arms.*)

PRIEST 1: Oh no. Did the pigeons get in again?
(*Zechariah shakes head. Shows something big, then flaps some more.*)

PRIEST 2: Did you see an angel?
(*Zechariah nods and claps like in charades. People act amazed.*)

PRIEST 1: An angel! What can this mean?
   (*Exit People, Zechariah. Priests remove curtains and incense and place chair stage right. Exit.*)

Scene 2—Elizabeth and Zechariah's Home
(*At rise: Elizabeth sitting on chair with mixing bowl and spoon (dry cereal inside). Enter Zechariah.*)

ELIZABETH: (*Stands.*) Zechariah, you're home! Sit down—I have wonderful news! The Lord has answered our prayers, and I'm going to have a baby!
(*Zechariah takes bowl, nods calmly, and sits down. Eats cereal.*)

ELIZABETH: Aren't you surprised?
(*Zechariah shakes head.*)

ELIZABETH: Aren't you going to say anything?
(*Zechariah shakes head.*)

ELIZABETH: I suppose you have the baby's name picked out too.
> (*Zechariah nods. Elizabeth looks puzzled. Exit.*)

Scene 3—Mary's Home
(At rise: Mary sweeping.)

NARRATOR: Six months later, God sent the angel Gabriel to Nazareth, a town in Galilee, to a young woman named Mary, who was engaged to a man named Joseph.
(*Enter Gabriel.*)

GABRIEL: Greetings, favoured lady! The Lord is with you.

MARY: (*Drops broom.*) What do you mean?

GABRIEL: Don't be afraid, Mary, for God has decided to bless you wonderfully. You will have a baby boy, and you will name Him Jesus. He will be very great. He will rule over Israel forever, and His kingdom will never end.

MARY: How will I have a baby? I'm not married.

GABRIEL: The Holy Spirit will come to you, and the power of God will cover you, and your baby will be the holy Son of God. (*Mary falls to her knees.*)

GABRIEL: Your relative Elizabeth is also going to have a son, even though she is very old. Everyone said she never would, but in three months she will. For nothing is impossible with God.

MARY: I am the Lord's servant. May everything you say come true.

> (*Exit Gabriel.*)

(Enter Mother.)

MOTHER: Mary, I heard voices. Who were you talking to?

MARY: An angel. I'm going to have a baby, the holy Son of God!

MOTHER: That's terrible! What will Joseph say?

MARY: Mother, you're not listening. The baby will be God's Son. God's.

MOTHER: You mean you will be the mother of the Messiah?

MARY: Yes.

MOTHER: How do you know for sure? Because people are going to find this very hard to believe.

MARY: The angel told me. The angel also said that your relative Elizabeth is expecting a baby.

MOTHER: Elizabeth is far too old to have a baby.

MARY: In three months she will have one.

MOTHER: All right, then. We will go to see Elizabeth and find out if this is true.

(Exit Mother and Mary.)

Scene 4—Elizabeth's Home

(At rise: Elizabeth sitting on chair. Baby inside her coat so she looks visibly pregnant. People behind her on both sides. Priest with a tablet and quill. Enter Mother and Mary.)

MOTHER: Greetings, Elizabeth.
(*Elizabeth stands up, visibly pregnant.*)

MOTHER: It's true!

ELIZABETH: How lovely of you to come see me!

MOTHER: Do you remember my daughter Mary?

MARY: Greetings, Elizabeth.
(*Elizabeth clutches her stomach as baby leaps for joy.*)

SONG: (*Tune of "Ding Dong Merrily on High." Elizabeth and Mary sing verses. Everyone except Zechariah sing 'Glorias.'*)

ELIZABETH: (*Singing.*) Oh Mary, you are greatly blessed, as is that boy of yours/ Why honour me by coming here, young mother of my Lord?

EVERYONE: Glooo-ooo-ooo-ooo-ooo-oria. Hosanna in the highest.

ELIZABETH: For when your greeting reached my ears, my baby leapt for joy. How blessed are you who have believed, God's word about your boy.

EVERYONE: (*'Gloria' as before.*)

MARY: My soul rejoices in the Lord, for He has chosen me! All generations will recall, His love to those who fear.

EVERYONE: (*'Gloria' as before.*)

MARY: He tosses rulers from their thrones, but lifts the humble high. He fills the hungry with good things, but to the rich, good-bye!

159

EVERYONE: (*'Gloria' as before.*)

MARY: He helps His servant, Israel; His arm does mighty deeds. To Abraham and all his kin, His promises He keeps.

EVERYONE: (*'Gloria' as before.*)
(*People crowd around Elizabeth, hiding her from view to end scene.*)

Scene 5—Three Months Later
(*At rise: Elizabeth sitting with the baby in her arms. Zechariah behind her. Crowd has moved aside, including priests (one with writing tablet and quill). Mary, Mother, and persons with lines are part of crowd.*)

NARRATOR: Three months later, Elizabeth's son was born. After eight days, they circumcised the child, according to the Law of Moses.

PERSON 1: What a beautiful baby.

PERSON 2: It's a miracle! Praise God.

PRIEST 1: His name shall be Zechariah, just like his father.

ELIZABETH: No! His name is John.

PRIEST 2: John? You don't have any relatives named John.

PRIEST 1: Why don't we ask his father?

PRIEST 2: His father can't speak.

PRIEST 1: Here is a writing tablet.

PRIEST 2: (*Speaking slowly and using sign language.*) Zechariah, what do you want to name your son? (*Zechariah takes tablet and writes. Gives it to Priest 1.*)

PRIEST 1: It says, "His name is John." (*Everyone gasps.*)

ZECHARIAH: The angel said to name him John! (*Everyone gasps again.*)

PERSON 3: He can speak!

PERSON 4: It's a miracle!

SONG: (*Same tune as before. Zechariah sings verses; everyone sings 'Glorias.'*)

ZECHARIAH: Praise to the God of Israel, for He has sent salvation. As prophets said so long ago, to make a holy nation.

EVERYONE: Glooo-ooo-ooo-ooo-ooo-oria. Hosanna in the highest.

ZECHARIAH: And you, my child, will go ahead; prepare the way for Him. God's rising sun will light the dark, shine tender mercy in.

EVERYONE: (*'Gloria' as before.*)

PRIEST 2: What will this child grow up to be?

(*Exit all.*)

Scene 6—Joseph's Home

NARRATOR: Mary returned home to tell Joseph her wonderful news.

(Enter Joseph.)

JOSEPH: I don't believe it! I can't marry Mary if she's already having a baby. I'll have to break our engagement. But it's too late tonight. I'll do it in the morning. *(Joseph lies down and goes to sleep. Enter Gabriel.)*

GABRIEL: Joseph, don't be afraid to marry Mary. Her baby is from the Holy Spirit. *(Exit.)*

JOSEPH: *(Wakes up.)* Wow. I guess I do believe it after all. God really is with her—and me.

(Exit.)

Scene 7—Bethlehem

NARRATOR: In those days, the emperor Caesar Augustus declared that everyone should return to his hometown to be put on the tax list. Joseph took Mary with him to Bethlehem. While they were there, the time came for her baby to be born. She had a son, wrapped him in swaddling clothes, and laid him in a manger, because there was no room for them at the inn.
(During narration, Joseph and Mary enter. Joseph places manger in front of chair. Mary sits.)

NARRATOR: There were shepherds living in the fields nearby, keeping watch over their flocks by night.
(Enter Shepherds and Sheep. Enter Head angel. Shepherds look afraid.)

HEAD ANGEL: Don't be afraid! I bring wonderful, joyous news for all people. This very day, your Saviour has been born in Bethlehem! You will find the baby wrapped up and lying in a manger.

(Enter all angels.)

SONG: *(Angels sing to the tune of "Jingle Bell Rock." Some angels dance while the others sing.)*

ANGELS: Gloria, Gloria, Glory to God! Your Saviour is here; sing songs of good cheer.

Wonderful Counsellor, Mighty God, Peace on Earth, good will towards all!

Gloria, Gloria, Glory to God! From high on His throne, He sends us His own.

A babe in a manger wrapped up snug and tight, on this Christmas night!

Sing His praises! God amazes! Clap your hands for joy!

Sing His glory! What a story! *(Clap.)* God Almighty in a tiny boy.

Gloria, Gloria, Glory to God! Peace and good will to all.

Sing His praises; Dance for joy—

(Clap.) Glory, Gloria! *(Clap.)* Glory, Gloria! *(Clap.)* Glory, Glory to God! *(This line three times.)*

(Exit Angels.)

SHEEP/SHEPHERDS: *(Recite poem all together.)*
Did you hear? Did you hear? The wonderful news?
Our Saviour has come as a baby today.
We must go and find Him. Come on, sheep, let's go!
We must find the baby asleep on the hay.

163

Do you see? Do you see? The wonderful child?
He's right where the angel told us He would be!
We must spread the news all around when we go.
Praise God for the Saviour He sent you and me.

OPTIONAL SONG: (*Shepherds and Sheep sing "Away in a Manger."*)

(*Exit Shepherds and Sheep.*)

Scene 8—Temple

NARRATOR: Forty days after Jesus was born, Joseph and Mary took Him to the temple to present Him to God and offer a sacrifice. The temple was a busy place, and Mary and Joseph didn't expect people to notice them. But two people did. (*During narration, Mary picks up baby and stands. Joseph moves manger and chair out of the way. Enter people, Simeon, and Anna.*)

SIMEON: I'm Simeon. May I hold your child? (*Mary hands baby to Simeon and he looks up.*) Lord, You promised me I wouldn't die until I saw Your Messiah, and today You have kept Your promise. (*To Mary and Joseph.*) God bless you, youngsters.

JOSEPH: That's amazing!

ANNA: My turn! My turn! (Takes the baby.) I am Anna, a prophet. Praise God for this wonderful child! Listen every-one. Look at this baby. This is the One who will redeem Jerusalem!

(*Anna walks around showing baby to everyone during narration. Gives back to Mary just before song.*)

NARRATOR: Some time later, Magi from the east came following a star and bringing gifts. Then an angel told Joseph to take Mary and the baby and flee to Egypt, because King Herod wanted to kill the new baby King. Joseph and Mary fled with Jesus and were safe. Mary treasured all these signs that God was with her.

Baby John grew up and became John the Baptist. When Jesus was 30 years old, John baptized Him in the Jordan River. For three years, Jesus taught and healed, and many people believed He was the Messiah. Then He was killed, but God raised Him from the dead: another sign, this time for the whole world. Now, Jesus sends His Holy Spirit to everyone who believes in Him, and comes wherever people gather in His name.

God is with us. Do not be afraid.

EVERYONE: Glooo-ooo-ooo-ooo-ooo-oria. Hosanna in the highest. (*Tune: chorus of "Ding Dong Merrily on High."*)

THE END

Story and Scriptures adapted from Luke 1, 2:1-38.
"Do not be afraid, for I am with you" – Genesis 26:24,
Deuteronomy 20:1, 31:6,8, Joshua 1:9, Isaiah 41:10,13,14,
Jeremiah 1:8, 42:11, Zechariah 8:15, and others

165

Christmas: Reflections on Christ's Coming

by

Marnie Pohlmann

The Coming
Luke 1:26-42 and Luke 2:1-6

Advent
A time of anticipation.
A time we plan how we will celebrate.
A time we decorate to share our joy.
A time we gather with family and friends, and even strangers.
A time we look for ways to give, as God commands, to widows and orphans.
A time we act in love to one another.

Our preparations are proper and good—even unbelievers appreciate joining in these festivities and they, too, practice kindness for others.
Yet there is more.
There is more to the advent, the waiting, than the parties and presents.
There is more than preparing for and enjoying gatherings.
There is even more than generosity and showing love.

There is the coming of the King.

Advent
A time to journey along with Mary and Joseph.
A time to be counted among God's people.
A time to announce, like the angels, the Good News.
A time to find shelter and safety in chaos.
A time to labour in new Life.

The Coming.
Advent is a time of preparation for the coming of the King.
Prepare your mind, your heart, your self for the coming.

The Arriving
Luke 2:7-18

Christmas Eve.
The night Joseph found shelter for Mary, who was in labour.
The night the Holy babe was born.
The night the angels announced to the shepherds, "Seek the baby in swaddling clothes, lying in a manger."
The night the shepherds obeyed the call, left their flocks, and found the Messiah.
The night angel choirs rejoiced in praise of God's presence on earth to bring peace to mankind.

Christmas Day.
The day we have been anticipating.
The day Hope came to live among us.
The day we found God, present in our ordinary lives.
The day the shepherds began to tell the Good News.

Arriving.
The day for which we have been preparing has come.
In the dark of the night, we wait.
We wait not for presents to be placed under the tree, or for stockings to be hung by the fire.
In the dark of the night, the babe has been born.

In the dark of the night, we find the Messiah.
In the dark of the night, we begin to praise God for
coming to us.

The Arriving.
In the light of Christmas day, we celebrate not presents
given and received, like the world celebrates, but
the Love given by God for mankind.
In the light of Christmas day, like the angel choirs, we
celebrate the arrival of our King.
In the light of Christmas day, like the shepherds, we share
the Good News.

The Arriving.
Christmas is a time to celebrate the fulfillment of God's Promise.
Seek God, who is present with you. Find God, who will change
your life. Share your excitement of meeting Emmanuel.

The Going
Luke 2:20 and Matthew 2:1-12

Going.
Returning to our ordinary life.
When we put away the decorations and reminders of the season.
When family and friends leave, returning to their ordinary days.
When our days return to daily chores, at home and work
and church.
When life settles into its routine.

As our world returns to ordinary life after Christmas,
believers do not return the same from the birth of Jesus.
We take the celebration of "God with us" into our lives, for
God is WITH us.
God is with us at home and work and church.
God is with us as we become busy with chores and playtimes.

God is with us, and His presence makes a difference in our ordinary lives.

Ordinary Time.
Like the shepherds, the lowly, we return to our lives changed.
Like the wise men, men of high standing, we bow in worship.
Like the wise men, no matter how long our journey to find Jesus, we offer God gifts and service.
Like the wise men, we are obedient to God's direction.
Like the wise men, we return to influence our own families, neighbourhoods, and countries, so that in God's timing, He will be known throughout the world.

The Going.
The celebration has not ended for those who have met God.
After the Christmas season is the time of following God each day.
Days of worship.
Days of training.
Days of sharing.
The celebration has just begun.

The Going.
Ordinary time is anything but ordinary.
Live, and share the coming of the King, the babe in the manger.

The Coming Again
1 Thessalonians 5:1-11, 23-24

The Second Advent
Now is the time for watching.
Now is the time for anticipation.
Now is the time for preparation.
Now is the time to offer shelter and safety in chaos.
Now is the time to share Good News.

Our lives are changed by the Coming, the Arriving, The Going found in the birth, the life, the death, the resurrection of Christ.
The Messiah has come.
The Messiah defeated death.
We are made righteous before God.
Yet in our ordinary lives, this is not the end.
There is more.

There is the return of the King.

Another waiting. Another preparation.
A time to journey along with other believers.
A time to be counted among God's people.
A time to announce the Good News.
A time to labour for God's Kingdom.
A time to prepare the Bride.

Coming Again.
The Second Advent is a time of preparation for the coming of the King.
Prepare your mind, your heart, your self for the coming.

BIOGRAPHIES
OF
AUTHORS
PHOTOGRAPHERS
&
EDITORS
&
A History of
InScribe Christian
Writers' Fellowship

Biographies

Authors & Photographers

Tandy Balson was born and raised in Vancouver, British Columbia. She and her husband now live on the outskirts of Calgary, Alberta. Tandy's greatest joys include spending time with family and friends, meaningful volunteer work, time in nature, reading, and writing. Tandy has been doing inspirational speaking in Western Canada since 2001. She is the author of two books, one of which was a finalist for The 2016 Word Awards in the inspirational book category. Tandy posts inspirational messages twice a week on her website blog and can be heard weekly on HopeStream Radio. Learn more at www.timewithtandy.com.

Kim Louise Clarke became interested in writing in 2010. She's found her niche in creative non-fiction and has had several essays and devotionals published. Her first book, *The French Collection – Moments with God in Paris*, published in 2016, was short listed for the 2015 Canadian Women's Journey of Faith contest. Kim lives in Calgary, Alberta with her husband. They have two adult children. She is a member of InScribe Christian Writers' Fellowship and has a Bachelor of Religious Education Degree from Prairie Bible Institute. Visit Kim at www.kimlouiseclarke.com.

Lynne Collier is a writer of fantasy, fiction, and non-fiction. She is also a Lay Associate Pastoral Counsellor and Christian Life Coach. Lynn's first published book was

Raising Benjamin Frog—A Mother's Journey With Her Autistic Son. Recent projects include writing courses for White Rose Writers school, and a *Novel Author's Workbook*, available in White Rose Writers' Etsy shop. Lynn lives in Ontario with husband, Stephen, their cat, Smokey, and a plethora of wildlife.

Patricia A. Earl is a retired kindergarten teacher and childcare giver. As a freelance writer, she has been a member of Inscribe Christian Writers' Fellowship for several years. She is the devotional editor of *Eternal Ink*, a Christian e-zine. Pat is married with three grown children and five grandchildren. Her hobbies are quilting and knitting, and she likes to work in the garden and bake. She is an elder at Knox Presbyterian Church in Manotick, Ontario where she plays keyboard with the praise team, sings in the choir, and leads the pastoral care team.

L. Marie Enns was born and raised as a preacher's kid on a Saskatchewan homestead. She accepted Christ at Vacation Bible School. An avid student, she went on to high school, bible school, teachers' college, and university. She became a teacher and married a teacher. They have four children, two children-in-law, and five grandchildren. After retiring, Marie enjoyed leading ladies' bible studies and Moms and Tots Sunday School classes. Her interests are family and friends, reading non-fiction and historical fiction, writing poetry and devotionals, listening to sacred and classical music, and singing. She and three friends alternately write the newspaper *Meditation Moments.*

Alvin Ens is a writer of prose and poetry, a writing mentor, and an editor. A member of two local writers' groups, Fraser Valley Poets Society and Fraser Valley Christian Writers, and a member of Inscribe Christian Writers' Fellowship and The Word Guild, Alvin has a wealth of experience in writing, editing, and teaching writing skills. He was a high school English teacher where he edited the creative writing magazine, advised the annual yearbook, and chaired the English Department. He freelances for both Christian and secular publications. He is a member of Level Ground Mennonite Church, Abbotsford, British Columbia.

Kathleen Friesen writes contemporary stories of faith that are about overcoming tough trials and deep heartaches. Her desire is for her readers to see themselves in the characters of her stories and to realize that Jesus Christ is the true hero of their lives. Kathleen spent her childhood in the Pacific Northwest and, after marrying the man of her dreams, survived the first thirty years of married life on the Canadian Prairies, where they raised three fantastic children. Now she and her patient husband, Ron, live in the beautiful Okanagan Valley of British Columbia.

Donna Gartshore wrote her first story at age five, about two friends who went on a picnic and saw a squirrel. She didn't use any punctuation! Better-punctuated stories have been published in *Spring Literary Magazine, Wascana Review,* and on CBC radio. She has also published poetry in *The Western Producer, Western People*, and *Seventeen Magazine*, and has written devotionals for *Eternity for Today.* One of her devotionals won first place and a poem won second place in the 2016 InScribe Christian Writers' Fellowship Fall Contest. Her first novel, published through the *Love Inspired* line of Harlequin, will be released in January 2018.

Pat Gerbrandt was delighted by stories about her parents' early years of marriage. When *Christian Week* asked her to write the "Senior Focus" column, she learned to enjoy biographical writing. She began her memoir after presenting life-story workshops to seniors' groups. *The Carillon, Manitoba Co-operator, Canadian Home Trends*, and *Fellowship Focus* have published her articles. Pat is writing more devotionals for *The Upper Room* now that a submission has been slated for print. Copy editing projects include theological training books, webpage content for a European software developer, and biographies. She delights in sharing stories of God's work.

Gloria Guest's interest in writing was first piqued in her grade twelve year when she placed first for Alberta in a national writing contest, receiving a scholarship and her story published in a small book. Since then her writing experience has mainly been in the newspaper industry as a reporter/columnist for various community newspapers. She has also received a certificate from the Institute of Children's Literature, Connecticut, USA and taken creative writing classes from the University of Toronto, with an interest in pursuing her certificate. Gloria blogs at gloriaguest@wordpress.com, offering words of hope, comfort, and healing.

Sharon Hamilton grew up in the mountains of British Columbia, in a small town that no longer exists. After she moved to Saskatchewan, she started writing stories about places that only exist in her imagination. She writes picture books, novels, and poems and has two published books, a picture book and a young adult fantasy novel. She has written several plays for the children and adults at her church. You can find her at http://sharonplumb.ca.

As a speaker, writer, and storyteller, **Carol Harrison** is passionate about mentoring people of all ages and abilities to help them find their voice and reach their fullest potential. She knows firsthand that life does not always go the way we plan or expect. She shares real life experiences combined with truths from God's Word to encourage others and point them to the hope God offers. Carol is a wife of one, mother of four adult children, and grandmother to twelve. She makes her home in Saskatoon, Saskatchewan.

Katherine Kavanagh Hoffman currently writes in Edmonton, Alberta. Christmas is one of her very favourite times of the year, and she is thrilled to be a contributor for this anthology. Some of her other favourite "things" are her husband, Kent, her two grown daughters and their partners, and her baby granddaughter, Elizabeth. Katherine is a transplanted Montrealer, who has also enjoyed living on the west coast, where she studied at Regent College and received her Master of Christian Studies in 1990. Katherine occasionally blogs at kgehca.blogspot.ca.

Elaine Ingalls Hogg is an inspirational speaker and award-winning author who lives near Sussex, New Brunswick. In addition to her books, her stories may be found on various websites and blogs, in more than two-dozen anthologies, in magazines and newspapers, and on the radio. Elaine has given writing workshops at schools, at Write! Canada, Write! Maritimes, and Kingswood University. She has also shared her faith and given inspirational talks at seniors' groups, service clubs, Christian Women's Clubs, and literacy and library events. Elaine shares her desk with two adopted rag-doll cats, Angus and Alex.

Connie Inglis is a missionary with Wycliffe Bible Transla-tors. She has spent much of the last 25 years in Southeast Asia with her husband and children serving as a literacy specialist, teacher, and editor. Connie has blogged about overseas living and has blogged her poetry since 2009. She has had both poetry and short stories published. Connie has been a member of InScribe Christian Writers' Fellowship since 2011 and is active in her InScribe writers' group, Writers Café. She is passionate about all-things-art especially poetry, about Jesus and seeing Him in day-to-day happenings, and about family, particularly her grandchildren.

Pastor Bob Jones is a recovering perfectionist who collects Coca-Cola memorabilia and drinks iced tea. His office walls are adorned with his sons' framed football jerseys, and his library shelves, with soul food. He has served churches as a pastor in Ontario, Quebec, and Alberta for nearly four decades. His passion is shepherding families through the highs and heartaches of life. Bob is a communicator, excelling in preaching, and is now making his mark as an author. Bob has been married to Jocelyn for 38 years, and is a father of two and grampa of four. He is a marathoner and is devoted to running his race of life as a champion.

Tracy Krauss is a multi-published novelist, playwright, and artist with several award winning and best selling novels, stage plays, devotionals, and children's books in print. Her work strikes a chord with those looking for thought provoking, faith based fiction laced with romance, suspense, and humor—no sugar added. She holds a Bachelor of Education from the University of Saskatchewan and has lived in many remote and interesting places in Canada's far north. She and her husband currently reside in beautiful British Columbia where she continues to pursue all of her creative interests. http://tracykrauss.com *Fiction on the edge – without crossing the line.* Contact: tracy@tracykrauss.com.

Gladys Krueger felt an early interest in writing. She has published poetry, children's stories, and a column for youth in her western Canadian church's paper. However, teaching in

Regina and Camrose plus marriage interrupted major writing time. In 2012 she published her first novel *False Love, True Love*. She and her husband, Wally, have been married nearly 56 years. They have two children and two grandchildren—a soccer player and a rock climber.

Sandra Lammers has always loved writing. She has taken many writing courses and has discovered that one of her favourite genres is children's stories. She also likes to take everyday events and spin them into devotionals and meditations. "Christmas Chaos" is her first real published piece. She grew up in southern British Columbia where she and her husband, Mark raised their two now-adult sons. Due to Mark's work, they have lived in the Naas Valley and Powell River, and currently reside in Fort St. John.

Marcia Lee Laycock is an award-winning writer and sought-after speaker. Having lived a few kilometres from the Arctic Circle, and two degrees off the Equator, Marcia draws from a rich field of experience. Marcia was the winner of the Best New Canadian Christian Author Award for her novel, *One Smooth Stone*, and she has published four devotional books and a fantasy series, which have also garnered awards. Marcia lives in central Alberta with her pastor husband. They have three grown daughters and two massive Great Dane grand-puppies. Discover more about Marcia's writing and speaking on her website www.marcialeelaycock.com.

Brenda C Leyland and her husband, Rick, live in northerly Alberta. Ever a seeker of beauty, she sees God's handiwork everywhere. A late bloomer to writing, Brenda finally sees that she had to live a longish life before she could write about how she found her beautiful life, first as a single woman for twenty years, and then as a happily married wife. When she's not writing, she and her husband are tearing up their garden to create something new and beautiful. They travelled recently through England and hope to return soon. You can find Brenda at beautiful.wordfromhome.com.

Wendy L. Macdonald is an inspirational writer, blogger, and podcaster who also loves to photograph nature on Vancouver Island. Besides writing and gardening, Wendy also enjoys hiking with her husband. She home schooled her three children and believes years of reading classics aloud developed her love of storytelling. She hopes you will visit her "Daily Bread" style Facebook, Twitter, and Instagram accounts. Her by-line is: "My faith is not shallow because I've been rescued from the deep." Samples of her photography are included in the 2017 Canadian anthology *Good Grief People*. Her website is www.wendylmacdonald.com, where she enjoys interacting with readers.

L. L. MacLellan is the author of the recently published inspirational novel *Somergate: The Scent of Autumn Roses*. She won her first literary award, a shiny blue ribbon, for a short story entered in a three-state regional writing contest back in the sixth grade, and has been writing ever since. Lori lives on Vancouver Island, British Columbia with her Mountie husband and their four beautiful daughters, where she cares for her mother and spends any free time gardening, antiquing, and, of course, writing.

M. Eleanor Maisey is a retired teacher who lives in Lethbridge, Alberta. Her membership in Inscribe Christian Writers' Fellowship plus correspondence writing courses helped inspire her to write articles and profiles of ordinary people doing special things for others. Some of these were published in Christian and secular magazines across Canada.

Born in East Germany, **Tina Markeli** was five when her family moved to Canada. She started school in a one-room schoolhouse in Saskatchewan but the family soon moved to Vancouver. There she came to know God personally. After graduation from the BC Institute of Technology, she served in the laboratory of a small mission clinic in Haiti where she met her husband. Together they worked in a Southeast Asian country where they raised two daughters, taught in a Bible College, and mentored church planters. Helmut and Tina have retired in Edmonton, Alberta.

Sally Meadows is a six-time national/international award-nominated author, singer/songwriter, and speaker from Saskatoon, Saskatchewan. Sally writes in a range of genres, from children's books and inspirational songs to short stories (fiction and non-fiction) for adults and magazine articles. She is also a photographer. Sally is a former teacher and enjoys sharing her knowledge about writing and song writing at workshops and conferences. She also raises awareness about autism through her picture book *The Two Trees*. Sally is the Press Coordinator for InScribe Christian Writers' Fellowship and the Saskatchewan representative for WIMM (Association of Christian Women in Music & Media) Canada. Visit Sally at https://sallymeadows.com.

Nina Faye Morey is a freelance writer, editor, and speaker from Saskatoon, Saskatchewan. She has had fiction, non-fiction, poetry, and art published in Christian, secular, and literary journals. She also contributed to InScribe's 2015 anthology, *7 Essential Habits of Christian Writers*. Nina has served as columns editor for InScribe's *FellowScript* magazine and is currently the editor-in-chief. Working with fellow writers through *FellowScript* and facilitating InScribe workshops brings her immense satisfaction. She also posts regularly on the *InScribe Writers Online* blog. Her other memberships include the Saskatchewan Writers' Guild and Saskatoon's Innovative Toastmasters Club. She enjoys visiting her grandchildren, reading, walking, and travelling.

Pamela Mytroen takes inspiration from the never-changing bedrock of God's Word, and the ever-changing skies and seasons of Saskatchewan. The tenacity of her English students, and the diverse cultures they represent, challenge her comfortable life and has informed many recent stories. She loves a tall Norwegian farm boy who has tried teaching her how to hunt, call coyotes, and check the gas gauge. Their four children and two grandchildren, LadyBug and Sir Cricket, offer a steady supply of sweet words, which she unabashedly plagiarizes and tucks into short fiction, blogs, human-interest pieces, and devotional writing.

Steph Beth Nickel is a communicator: she is a freelance writer and editor; one of the producers for HopeStreamRadio; and regularly guest blogs for a number of sites. She is in the process of putting together the *To Nurture and Inspire* series of ebooks. She is the coauthor of the award-winning *Living Beyond My Circumstances*, Paralympian Deb Willows's memoir. Deb and Steph have begun work on a follow-up volume, *Still Living Beyond My Circumstances*. Steph is an active member of InScribe Christian Writers' Fellowship and The Word Guild.

Kimberley Payne is a motivational speaker and author. Her writings relate to raising a family, pursuing a healthy lifestyle, and everyday experiences in building a relationship with God. Visit Kimberley at www.kimberleypayne.com.

Marnie Pohlmann shares her heart at *Phosphorescent* (https://marniewriter.com/) passionately showing the Light of God in dark times. She draws on her own experience with childhood sexual abuse, cancer, post-traumatic stress disorder, depression, and the joys of marriage, parenting, and life in the north. She regularly contributes to *Inscribe Writers Online*, has published articles and poetry in various online and print magazines, and has spoken at ladies' events. Marnie writes from northern British Columbia where she provides administrative support to our Canadian heroes in red serge and joins her husband in pastoring Taylor's Peace Community Church.

Jack Popjes and his wife, Jo, worked in Brazil for 24 years, completing the linguistic, literacy, and Bible translation program among the Canela people in 1990. They travelled for two years in a mini-motorhome throughout North America, speaking at hundreds of churches, conferences, and promotional events. Jack then served as president of Wycliffe Canada for six years and of Wycliffe Caribbean for three years. Wycliffe published three books of his story-based columns. He is now writing volume two of a four-volume autobiography. Jack and Jo have three married daughters and eight grandchildren ranging in age from 17 to 26.

Charleen Raschke and her husband John live in Edmonton, Alberta. They have three adult children. Their youngest son continues to live with them long term as they care for his many needs. Charleen's hope is to encourage many hearts to not give up, no matter how difficult life is. She has authored *A Season of Ashes* and writes devotionals for those going through pain.

Ruth A.M. Sakstad is an avid reader and an aspiring writer. Ruth is currently working on a murder mystery as well as a collection of poems. She resides in Edmonton, Alberta.

Carol Schafer's publishing experience began with poems and articles when she was a teenager. Much more recently, she has published three children's storybooks: *Lorenzo's Incredible Leap: A Story of Courage* (Word Alive, 2012), *Grison, the Grumpy, Grouchy Island Goat: A Story of Healthy Choices* (Word Alive, 2013), and *Cloddia's Desert Dance: A Story of Finding Your Place* (Word Alive, 2016). Until 2013, Carol was an academic editor at Athabasca University. She holds a BA in English Literature from Athabasca University, two diplomas from The Institute of Children's Literature, and a Master of Practical Ministry diploma from Wagner Leadership Institute Canada.

A member of InScribe Christian Writers' Fellowship since 1998, **Janet Seever** is a staff writer for Wycliffe Bible Translators and lives in Calgary, Alberta. She is the wife of Dennis, and the mother of two adult children, one of who is married. Her nine-year-old grandson, Andrew, is a joy in her life. She enjoys writing inspirational stories and has written articles for *CSC News*, a publication of Centre Street Church, since 2008.

Ruth Smith Meyer is the author of two adult novels, *Not Easily Broken* and *Not Far from the Tree*, a children's book, *Tyson's Sad Bad Day*, and her memoir, *Out of the Ordinary*. She has had her work published in six anthologies including the *Hot Apple Cider* series. As an inspirational speaker, Ruth has resourced many diverse groups. Throughout her life she has been active and provided leadership in her church and community and as a presenter for Marriage Encounter. She lives in Ailsa Craig, Ontario and is the parent/step-parent of eight children, eighteen grandchildren, and six great-grandchildren.

Ruth L. Snyder resides close to Glendon, Alberta with her husband, five children, and a husky/malamute named Olaf. Ruth enjoys writing articles, devotionals, short stories, and Christian fiction. She is a member of The Creativity Coaching Association, The Christian PEN, and serves as President of InScribe Christian Writers' Fellowship. Ruth loves her job teaching Music for Young Children and private piano lessons. She also enjoys speaking about what she's learning in her walk with God, as a parent, and as a writer. In her spare time, Ruth enjoys reading, crafts, volunteering, photography, and travel. Find out more at http://ruthlsnyder.com.

Sandra Somers is a former teacher and instructor of English as a Second Language. She has lived in Alberta and Colombia, South America. Her devotionals and award-winning inspirational articles have appeared in such publications as *FellowScript*, T*he Christian Communicator,* and *The Upper Room Disciplines*. She also contributes regularly to the *InScribe Writers Online* blog. Sandra is a member of InScribe Christian Writers' Fellowship and The Word Guild. She resides in Calgary, Alberta.

Terrie Todd is an award-winning author who has published three historical novels (*The Silver Suitcase, Maggie's War,* and *Bleak Landing*), eight stories with *Chicken Soup for the Soul,* two stage plays with *Eldridge Plays and Musicals,* and numerous articles for *FellowScript*. She's been a member of Inscribe Christian Writers' Fellowship since 2000. After twenty years leading a church drama team, Terrie now works part-time as an Administrative Assistant at City Hall. She lives with her husband, Jon, in Portage la Prairie, Manitoba, where they raised their three children. You can follow Terrie's shenanigans at www.terrietodd.blogspot.com.

Editors

Janis Cox is a member of InScribe Christian Writer's Fellowship, The Word Guild, and American Christian Fiction Writers. The award-winning author/illustrator of *Tadeo Turtle* and *The Kingdom of Thrim,* she also speaks in schools. Her Bible study, *A Companion Bible Study to Ed Hird's Battle for the Soul of Canada* is available on Amazon, as is *I Remember—The Seasons*, a book for caregivers of those with dementia, which she illustrated. Jan's talk "Growing Through God's Word" is podcast every Tuesday on HopeStreamRadio. Janis can be reached at www.janiscox.com and on Facebook, Pinterest, and Twitter as authorjaniscox.

Janice L. Dick is an award-winning InScribe Christian Writers' Fellowship member who writes from her rural home in Saskatchewan. She writes contemporary and historical fiction, blogs, book reviews, and inspirational articles. In September 2016, Janice became the first recipient of the prestigious Janette Oke award, presented by InScribe at their fall conference. In 2016, Janice established her indie imprint: Tansy & Thistle Press: faith, fiction, forum, and has since released two more historical novels. Find out more at https://janicedick.wordpress.com/.

A skilled editor and artistic coach, **Colleen McCubbin**'s passion is in artistic midwifery, drawing alongside women to provide expertise, strength, and assurance as their newly conceived literary life is nurtured and brought forth into the society of the wider world.

Sally Meadows is the Press Coordinator for InScribe Christian Writers' Fellowship and is the managing editor of this project. For more information about Sally, please see her biography above under Authors & Photographers.

Janet Sketchley is the author of the *Redemption's Edge* Christian suspense series and *A Year of Tenacity: 365 Daily Devotions*. Her novels have each been finalists in The Word Awards, and she's also a contributor to the *Hot Apple Cider* inspirational anthologies. Janet is an Atlantic Canadian writer who believes strongly in the importance of developing unity and community amongst Canadian Christians who work with words, coast to coast. She is a long-time member of InScribe Christian Writers' Fellowship and The Word Guild. Janet blogs about faith and books. She loves Jesus and her family, and enjoys reading, worship music, and tea.

Carolyn R. Wilker is an author, editor, writing instructor, and storyteller. Her publishing credits range from creative non-fiction, devotions, and poetry to her book, *Once Upon a Sandbox*, as well as other regional to international publications. Her work has appeared in *Good Grief People, Hot Apple Cider with Cinnamon*, and *Tower Poetry*. She has worked with speakers and authors on travel memoirs and business books, as well as books for children. A member of the Baden Storytellers' Guild, Carolyn has shared stories at The Button Factory, Heart and Hand Festival, World Storytelling Day concerts, and the Ark in Bridgewater, Nova Scotia.

A History of InScribe Christian Writers' Fellowship

by

Ruth L. Snyder

The Central Alberta Christian Writers began after twelve writers from Alberta attended the Decision School of Christian Writing in July 1979. June Bevan, Ruth Viske, and Sophie Thunell served on the executive.

The purpose was, "To provide a vehicle for mutual support, stimulation and growth for Christian writers in Alberta." The main objective was to sponsor an annual conference, with the first one held November 8, 1980, at the Canadian Lutheran Bible Institute, with sixty-six in attendance. The next year forty-two attended, with twenty-two paid members (fee of $15.00). The name was changed to Alberta Christian Writers' Fellowship in 1981. Early forms of advertising included interviews of Executive members on CKRD-TV (Red Deer) and articles in local papers.

Subsequent fall conferences took place at Camp Kuriakos, Lacombe Nazarene Church, Oriole Park Missionary Church, North American Baptist College, and the Grey Nuns Regional Centre. In October 1989, the tenth anniversary of ACWF was marked at the Hospitality Inn in Calgary.

Presidents over the years have been June Bevan (1 year), Sophie Thunell (2), Alice Cundiff (1), Sophie Stark (7), Lavyne Osbak (1), Gerald Hankins (2), Elsie Montgomery (6), Marcia Laycock (5), Eunice Matchett (3), Lisa Wojna (2), Jack Popjes (3), and Ruth L. Snyder (since Fall 2013).

The first writing contest deadline was June 30, 1983, with judges arranged by Alberta Culture. We now have two annual contests – the Fall Contest for unpublished pieces, with prizes awarded at conference, and the Winter Contest for published pieces.

The first writing group formed on September 15, 1986 at Barbara Mitchell's home. Currently there are fifteen local writing groups meeting across Canada.

In 1983, Helena Brown sent out the first single page ACWF Newsletter. Over the years, the newsletter matured into the present thirty-two-page *FellowScript* magazine.

Spring workshops began in April 1990 in Red Deer. In 1996 the name was changed to Spring WorDshop.

In the fall of 1996, ACWF expanded across Canada as ACWF-CanadaWide. In 1999 the name changed to InScribe Christian Writers' Fellowship. The same year the website, InScribe.org, began, along with a listserv on Yahoo.com, where members share questions, answers, successes, mistakes, prayer requests, and friendly greetings.

For the 20th Anniversary, Nathan Harms published *Companion*, with history and photos. Members were encouraged to contribute one page. The featured conference speakers were Phil Callaway, Linda Hall, Maxine Hancock, and Janette Oke.

In 2007, we began a blog at http://inscribewritersonline.blogspot.com for members to post and get feedback.

In 2010, *InScribed: 30 Years of Inspiring Writers*, a second anthology by InScribe members, was published.

In 2014 we began a second blog, http://inscribe.org/blog, where selected members share information about writing. The same year, Glynis Belec started regular online contests—Word Challenges—where writers receive a prompt and have one week to submit. Several of the contests have resulted in publishing opportunities.

We look back with gratitude, and continue to seek God's guidance as we stimulate, encourage, and support Christians who write.